MW00613263

THE CRYSTAL MOUNTAIN

As long as we struggle only with the problem of our everyday existence—food, work, health, and sex, we are not very much above the animals. We begin to be persons only when we start to wonder what life is all about.—Silone in "The Seed Beneath the Snow"

THE CRYSTAL MOUNTAIN

By Lucille Oliver

HERALD PUBLISHING HOUSE
Independence, Missouri

DEDICATION PAGE

I am a realist. Contrary to the title, this book is not about some imaginary mountain peak that houses a crystal castle. It's about the rugged miles we travel in this life, and the ability we need to see the beauty, joy, and potential around us.

It's about a Man who was born nearly two thousand years ago and whose influence still penetrates the choices we make, bringing awareness of the responsibilities which ultimately go with such choices.

It's about love—for ourselves, for God, and for those around us, without which we can never reach the peak of the mountain.

And it's about the dream of peace which is even now in the making.

To my children—Bob, Carol, and John whom I love very much, but who must climb their own mountains—I dedicate this book, and to my husband Lee, with whom I have traveled the valleys and peaks for thirty-five years.

There are many others who have helped me in my search whose lives have touched mine with music, beauty, and love. My deepest thanks to them, and to the One who ultimately taught me the way to the top of the mountain from which the Living Waters flow in a crystal stream of pure and radiant joy!

The Author

CONTENTS

PROLOGUE

I, a member of creation, sing the burning oneness binding everything. —Kenneth Boulding

Life is many things—a mountain to climb, a river to cross, a valley to walk—but it is more than this. It's power, energy, aliveness, belonging. It is exhilarating joy impregnated with poignant sorrow. I have reached the conclusion that all of us must climb our own mountains, ford our streams, face our valleys—alone and together—and through personal choices realize our special dream in relationship to all other people. Though each of us is a unique being, each is also a vital part of the whole.

I have discovered a plateau that we can reach in our individual lives to which we can go in hours of distress and grief—times when we feel alien and afraid. I call this my crystal mountain. It sustains me in the business of daily living. It enables me to sing the oneness of the universe.

I am an average person with average talents and skills, but because I have glimpsed the summit I have been made acutely aware of the focal point of life. If this can happen to me, it can also happen to others.

9

Notwithstanding conventional religion, which I confess at times has turned me off, I perceive that God (or whatever name may be given him) is at the helm of the universe. Through my significant personal experiences with the man called Jesus I have found my reason for being. I am a child of the universe. I am a part of every living thing, and nothing dies except a part of me dies also. I weep when I see the destruction of the earth as living trees, plants, and grass are slaughtered to make way for concrete jungles.

Yet nothing is born but there is newness in me. Nor will there ever be an end of me, for life is forever. Matter and energy which find expression in all living things continue in a never ending cycle. I'm sure the dimension will change, but I shall persist forever and continue to grow.

As I sat watching the ocean cresting with billowing whitecaps, my two-year-old grandson exclaimed, "Look, Grandmama, there's soap on the water!" Indeed it looked like mountains of suds cascading around us. Nearing dusk, the white sand looked like snow, but it was warm with gentle breezes blowing across our faces. We sat for a long time building sand castles, letting the sand sift through our hands and toes, and allowing the water to wash it smooth.

There are times when I can almost believe I came from the sea, because I love it so much. This particular place on the Gulf Coast of Florida is part of my crystal mountain, and the memory of it sustains me in times of loneliness and struggle. Nearly everyone has such a special place or time. Without realizing why, we each have a desperate need to belong, to have our own place in time and space. There are periods in my life when I cry out for the solitude and beauty of the ocean. If I shut my eyes and concentrate very hard, I can almost feel the breeze and the rhythm of the pulsating water lifting my spirits and washing away my weariness. At such times I seem to be strangely close to the Power of the universe and feel assured that I am never really alone.

As a child I was always fascinated by the glimmer of glass reflected in multicolored prisms hanging from chandeliers. Growing up, I found myself intrigued with glass of any kind or color. I began a collection—bottles, bowls, vases, lamps, sun-catchers of various kinds—some old and valuable, others inexpensive but just as delightful. Crystal has a special meaning for me, and as I began to visualize what a whole crystal mountain would mean I found myself wanting the same peace and beauty for all people. It had to be both visible and fancied. (We all need fantasy. Harvey Cox claims that losing the ability to fantasize results in a great loss of joy, beauty, and mystery.)

I was reared in a religious environment. My studies in college included credits in the Bible and history of the Scriptures. In my middle years, however, I began to perceive that organized religion just didn't produce all the answers it claimed to have. The results of the teachings of Christ were sorely lacking in the so-called "Christian society." I became aware of the manipulation of people within the structures of the organized bodies and of the self-righteousness which deadens the spirit. I began to see that each person must have more freedom to respond, to be himself, to grow to full potential, and that the choice must always remain his to accept or reject. The authoritarian institutional church seemed to me to demand compliance with too many rules and regulations which stifled the individual rather than freeing him as One had promised long ago.

I also became aware that a crystal mountain as I envisioned was possible for all persons, if they could become open to life and aware of the joy which is all around. I concluded that fear is the one deleterious element that prevents people from reaching full potential. It is both crippling to the heart and devastating in the search for the mountain.

The pages ahead reveal some facts I have discovered through my own experiences (what other source is viable?). I believe there is dawning an age of peace and brotherhood when all shall have access to their own crystal mountains.

Man, day-by-day, builds a world which never was before. This is creation. In fact, it is the co-creation of the ever-coming God and the ever-becoming man.

—Thomas R. Henry

Chapter 1
THERE WAS THIS CARPENTER'S SON. . . .

Jesus Christ, Jesus Christ,
Who are you, what have you sacrificed?
Jesus Christ, Superstar!
Do you think you're who they say you are?
— Jesus Christ, Superstar

Down through the ages great men and women like Plato, Socrates, Abraham, Confucius, Buddha, Mohammed, Madam Curie, Thomas Edison, and Isaac Newton have changed the lives of millions of people.

Nearly two thousand years ago, however, there was this carpenter's Son who actually influenced life on the earth more than any other single person. He was born in a remote village in Bethlehem. History records that his mother, Mary, was a young Jewish maiden in her early teens. Her husband, Joseph, was recognized as the earthly father of the child, but Mary denied that she had had sexual relationships with any man prior to the birth. Both were of the House of David and because of their lineage were required by law to travel from their home in obscure Nazareth to Bethlehem to render an accounting to the authorities.

It was during this trip that the time for the birth arrived. Since all the inns in the city were full that night, the baby was born in a stable. Though there isn't much historical record about the child after the age of twelve, it can be assumed that he was reared much as any Hebrew lad of that day.

In the thirtieth year of his life, however, something occurred that has made a significant impact on the world. This man called Jesus began a peace march along the dusty roads of Galilee. He kept company with odd people, many of whom were social misfits and outcasts. He began to have an unusual influence on the multitudes who followed him. He taught a unique doctrine about love and peace and the worth of every human being. He spoke of truth and freedom and the need to be a steward over life. He minimized material things and said man was a spiritual being. He encouraged those who followed him to move out in faith, to risk, to love, and to enjoy life.

Soon he became an object of grave concern among both Jewish and Roman authorities. Ultimately he brought down their wrath upon himself and his company of followers. The result was imprisonment and death by crucifixion just three years after he first began his march . . . but those three years revolutionized the earth. Time was divided; the calendar was changed; and his message of love resulted in dynamic input in each succeeding generation following his death. Added to this was the record of an empty tomb revealing some strange power which he evidently held over death.

One writer has said that all people believe in God, for everyone knows responsibility. Each has a name for God: truth, reality, ground of being, the unknown. . . . The question is not "Does God exist?" but "What is God like?" The answer comes in events and in the Event of Christ in history. There is no denying that Jesus of Nazareth existed, for history records that he did. The question here is "Has the Event of his life interposed itself into our lives, enabling us to overcome the misfortunes of which life is made?"

There is no "proof" of Christ, for "he is not in the area of academic argument." The verdict about Christ comes by faith. Faith is always response as a person comes face-to-face with mystery. All of us at some time wonder who we are, for what purpose we are here, and to what end we go. Life remains a mystery, despite modern technology and achievements.

Death stands, as always, the greatest threat to

our peace of mind. Failure to face it, speak of it, or think deeply about it does not eliminate it. We merely avoid a confrontation, until such time as we are deeply in its clutches and can think no more.

So we continue seeking. Answers only bring more questions. But as George Buttrick puts it so beautifully, "When we bring our real questions to him, the needle of our total life swings to him quiveringly and then settles, as a compass to the magnetic north."

Perhaps it isn't so important whether we believe in the Virgin Birth or the Resurrection (I happen to) but we do need to admit that the impact of this Man's life on the lives of people through the ages is of great significance. He taught earthlings how to gain power needed for daily living which would transcend life's sufferings and insure peace, joy, and love-filled personalities. He was the prime example of love incarnate—something no human fully understands. And his humanness brought the visible lesson that life's obstacles, heartaches, and hurts can be overcome and mended. His divinity which all humanity shares to a degree brings an added dimension which, if accepted, assures love and fulfillment.

There is a Book, which, while not absolute in

18

every instance, does give a few details of the actions of this Man. The Bible speaks of what he did, and how he did it. We know that he was a thorn in the flesh of the religionists of his day. He made statements like, "The Sabbath was made for man, not man for the Sabbath," indicating that the important thing was man, not the Sabbath. He presented no rules about what man should do on this day, for man controlled the day. He bitterly condemned self-righteousness. He ate with sinners and publicans, forgave adultery by pointing to the sins of the accusers, taught compassion and forgiveness, and said if one served his fellowmen he was actually in the service of God. He indicated that even a cup of water given to another would be rewarded. But the strangest teachings of all had to do with a kingdom which he said he came to bring—a kingdom not *of* this world but *in* this world—a kingdom not with armies of might and authoritarian power but a kingdom of peace and brotherhood which would make of earth the paradise it was created to be.

Although on one occasion he stated that he could command legions of angels to protect him, he refused to use force of any kind. He taught that if a person was slapped on one cheek he should turn the other for similar treatment. He spoke of going "the second mile." To those who had been steeped in the tradition of "an eye for an eye and a tooth for a tooth" this appeared to be heresy. How could man survive if he didn't obliterate his enemy? The Hebrews had been in slavery most of their lives, and they looked for a deliverer, a Messiah who would free them. But this man spoke of being free even though in chains. On one occasion he said that truth would free a man. But what did he mean by truth?

He taught further that all men are of equal importance in the sight of God, and he promised a power available to those who would seek and qualify for it. This power was to transform the old man into a new being—one capable of love and peace—and he likened it to putting new wine into new bottles.

This carpenter's Son came long ago, but the world has continued to hate and fight and bleed. Although there have always been some who have followed the man called Jesus, evidently not enough have followed his way with fidelity to bring about the sought-for peace and plenty which he promised and which, I believe, is possible.

The trouble isn't with the plan or the planner but with those who must implement the plan. Today the youth are singing, "Jesus Christ,

Superstar, do you think you're who they say you are?" They're asking the question, and wanting an answer. The example of those who have claimed to follow this man does not suffice. His life is again having renewed influence on odd companies of people, and the truth of his being is somehow being revealed again in depth. He is being taken out of candlelit, stained-glass sanctuaries into the streets of despair, the gutters of life, the garbage heaps (as where he was crucified). I'm confident this is where he wants to be, because he said he came to help those who had lost their way. We've put him on a golden cross and worshiped from afar, placating our conscience and feeling that we are followers of his way, but this has served only to crucify him afresh. I'm sure he walks the city streets today and agonizes over the depravity to which some have sunk, and in which others allow them to remain. He must cringe when he hears congregations singing, "My Jesus, I love thee," and then watch these same people walk from their chapels without noticing the lonely, the heartbroken, the forsaken, the lost. He must grieve as he witnesses the apathy which so-called Christians have toward his world which has been smothered in concrete—where men, because of their consuming passion for things, have polluted the air and streams. How he must weep at man's inhumanity to man, at the bitterness and hate which even those who claim to love exhibit in their daily lives.

Jesus proclaimed with authority, "The kingdom of God is within you, or has already come in your midst." Today we see little evidence of it. In my search I have discovered that many intellectuals are also proclaiming that such a kingdom shall be. They use different words, but the meaning is the same. The year 2000 promises to be something of a crossroads for humanity. Charles Reich calls it "the coming forth of a new consciousness." George Leonard refers to it as "transformation." But before any of these men were around there was this carpenter's Son.

Christianity has long promulgated the thesis that man is capable of transformation. It has been called by various names—new birth, the putting on of a new man, renewal, transformation, etc. Yet with only a few exceptions this dream has never actually materialized and then only for brief periods of time. There are one or two examples of such transformations cited in history when certain societies have existed in a comparative state of peace and prosperity. Men were transformed from selfish, greedy, lustful, inhuman entities into happy, joyful, concerned persons able to relish life, to enjoy and protect their environment, to relate to other living things, and to prosper in all areas of achievement. Such was possible because they grasped the love of a Creator and responded to one another as brothers. Their respect for all living things resulted in sharing rather than in manipulation.

Leonard writes:

It is my thesis that the current period is unique in history and that it represents the beginning of the most thorough-going change in the quality of human existence . . . since five thousand years ago. I also argue that most of our current troubles from free-floating anxiety to the breakdown of craftsmanship can be traced ultimately to the lack of a vivid unifying principle or belief system; the biblical dictum that where there is no vision the people perish is by no means merely metaphorical. The time is overdue for the emergence of a new vision of human and social destiny and being.

Today humanity is in the death throes searching for such a transformation. To those who care enough to search beneath the facade of a sophisticated society the cries of anguish for reconciliation—for completeness—can be heard around the earth. Fear has catapulted men into a demoralizing mass of inhumanity within their own ranks. They have been taught that increasing control of nature and the world has brought leisure and freedom, but they have not been told that control over the material world brings equivalent control of human beings. Men cannot control outer space until they have recognized and mastered inner space. Perhaps their consciousness has atrophied. Nevertheless, times are changing. People are beginning to wake up, to become aware of what life is really all about. As Leonard claims, "Awareness brings transformation."

From the moment of birth when the infant is forced out of the safe, secure world of its mother's womb, there is a perpetual longing to be an integral part of another human being and the universe which houses him for whatever period of time is allotted to him. Doctors tell us that a baby must have love—which includes touching and cuddling—if he is not to become an emotional cripple in his adult life. If he is denied this in infancy, he becomes unable to transform his life into the dream. This can be handed down from one generation to another because of the inability to love and respond to others.

Noel, my week-old granddaughter, had just come from the hospital. She was a good baby, but late in the night she began crying softly. I knew I would have only a short time with her, since my plane left early the next morning. (I had been caring for the two-year-old while my daughter was in the hospital.) When I picked the baby up and held her close to me she stopped crying at once. It was a magic moment as I felt the love and warmth of her tiny body against mine. It was a moment I would have prolonged—holding within my hands such wonderful, pulsating life—but I had to put her back in her crib and get my much-needed rest for the trip home.

At the office one day an employee with whom I was not well acquainted joined me for a coffee break. She began talking about her children, now in their late teens, who had said they would never bring children into such a world as the one we now face. I asked if this was because of the war, poverty, etc., but she said, "No, that isn't the reason. It's because they feel they could never be adequate parents. Their father is unable to be a good parent, and this has affected them." She continued, "They are determined to stop the cycle, for while their father has given them everything they need materially, he has been unable to give them the one thing they have craved—love and understanding." Evidently his lack was the result of denial in his own childhood.

How do we rectify such lack? Psychologists

are flinging volumes at us about how to find our place in the world, how to cope, how to like ourselves and others. All manner of encounter groups, sensitivity sessions, and dialogue therapy can be had for the asking, but more and more people continue to enter mental institutions daily. Suicides mount with increasing intensity and people continue to struggle with psycho-somatic diseases which Leonard appropriately calls "dis-ease." Many persons are at "dis-ease" with themselves, and no one seems to be able to help. Often the higher the intelligence, the more profound the student, the more tragic the lack. The man without faith is the most tragic of all men.

Eric Fromm said there were two kinds of persons—the creators and the destroyers. He used Greek terms: nekrophiles (lovers of dark-ness, destruction, and death), and biophiles (lovers of life, light, and love).

The great Pascal wrote that every man has to make a crucial wager—and he must make it by himself; either this marvelous earth is meaning-ful and purposeful, or it is a puzzling enigma, filled with arresting "sound and fury but signify-ing nothing."

Because of my personal relationship with Jesus which has enabled me to discover the joy and beauty of life, I would like to share my experiences in the pages ahead. Perhaps I can provide answers to some nagging questions: What does his life mean to us today? What about this peace march he began so long ago? Is it relevant for us? When the greatest minds of our age cannot produce the peace all men long for, is his plan worth a try?

There'll be days when you won't get very far in your climb. You may even fall behind, as I have often done. In fact, you may declare war on yourself, your companions, your children, and your fellow-workers. Battles are fought inside the heart and mind, and the anguish can never be relieved until people are willing to face their hostility and fear, propose a truce, and meet themselves at the conference table where peace strategy can begin. Can there ever be lasting peace on earth unless there is first peace in each heart?

I can assure you of one thing. You begin this climb up your mountain with a promise: there is Someone who loves you, just as you are, who lived and died for you and who offers you power unlimited to celebrate life with peace, joy, and love. When you make this discovery, you'll be overwhelmed.

Will you visualize a scene with me now? We're

standing on the shore by the Sea of Galilee. It's dusk, and the sun is sinking slowly. If we look closely, we can see a lone figure approach a group of men who are just coming in from fishing, pulling in the catch from their boat. One looks up and catches the eyes of the Stranger who speaks in commanding tones: "Follow me and I'll make you fishers of men." The men drop their nets and follow him.

Let's join them.

The central purpose of Christ's life is to destroy the life of loneliness and to establish here on earth the life of love.— Thomas Wolfe

Chapter 2

AT THE FOOT OF THE MOUNTAIN

Like you, I have been here since the beginning, and shall be until the end of days. There is no ending to my existence. For the human soul is but a part of a burning torch which God separated from Himself at Creation.—Ross Snyder

When I was three years old my father was killed. Left with two small daughters, Mother became bitter. While she had come from an active churchgoing family, she decided she just wouldn't attend anymore. I guess she blamed God for her misery.

One night she had a dream. She saw a great wheat field, and walking there was a man she thought to be Christ. Holding his hand was a small child who looked very much like me. He spoke to Mother. "You must go back to church, Olive, or Lucille will be lost."

This dream made a profound impression on her and she returned to church.

I was reared in the Christian faith. My father was Irish Catholic and Mother was brought up in the Southern Baptist Church, but they united in

29

the Christian Church after marriage. I heard all the familiar clichés about God being love. I sang with the other children, "Jesus loves me, this I know, for the Bible tells me so." I attended Sunday school, vacation church school, evangelistic meetings, etc. I was taught that smoking, drinking, and sex were wrong. Each Easter Mother made beautiful dresses for my sister and me.

When I was seven, Kate and I were placed in an orphan's home. I remember having to kneel by my bed each night and repeat with the other children, "God is my strength from day to day; God walks beside me, guides my way; I now am wise, I now am true, patient, kind and loving too; all things I am, can do and be, through Jesus Christ who lives in me." I'm not sure where this prayer came from but I still remember it. And while I didn't understand it fully, it must have given me some security.

I was eleven when I first responded to the hymn, "Just as I am, without one plea." I can recall walking alone down the long aisle of the church as the congregation sang. I was moved by it and felt I was ready for baptism, which called for making a public confession of faith and accepting Christ as my personal savior. I remember feeling happy. It was years later, however, before I truly understood the meaning of the words of this hymn . . . "just as I am, though tossed about, with many a conflict, many a doubt; fightings within and fears without, O Lamb of God, I come."

After high school I attended Midway College near Lexington, Kentucky, where I learned a great deal about climbing my mountain. My teachers were interested in me as an individual, and though discipline was strict, love and understanding were lavished on me by those dedicated women. Included in my courses were five years of Bible studies. I was always seeking to learn more about the man called Jesus and his way. I thought seriously of entering a seminary, but then decided to work for several years to help Mother, who had never remarried and who had worked hard to put my sister and me through school. At the end of this time, I began married life with a companion who was of another faith. After two years of investigating his church, I decided it was for me. I have never regretted the training I received as a child and youth; it has served as a good foundation upon which to build at later stages of my life. I have grown from a Christian who believed in a "don't do this" type of religion to one who believes, as did St. Augustine, "love and do as you please." The key word is love. If only we can learn to love people enough to free them to become what God intended they should, we'll discover our crystal mountain and be willing to help others discover theirs. When this happens, the world can be transformed into the paradise it once was and is destined to be again.

At fifty I still come just as I am—full of fear, guilt, and resentment—but with one big difference. I know myself much better now than I did as an eleven-year-old girl, and knowing myself, I am still assured that God loves me, even as I am. Nothing I can do will ever change that.

Despite the triteness of the quotes I learned in Sunday school, I am assured that God's very nature is love. This is something we just can't comprehend, try though we may. Even in our sin, he loves us and seeks us out. As human beings, we turn away from the sinner because of the sin. But God, while hating the sin, continues with great compassion to love the sinner. Because of this love, I am able to respond in varying degrees to his call and bit by bit purge my life of those things that keep me from total commitment to a better way of life.

I confess there are days now when I feel like saying to God, "Look, I've had it. I just don't want to be bothered with all the mess in the world. So please excuse me." Strange as it may seem, I often seem to hear him reply, "Yes, it does get tiring, doesn't it? But after you rest a bit, you'll be ready to go again." And sure enough, I am.

The sincere Christian of today will of necessity face the dilemma of the Christian faith: it just hasn't worked for enough people. Only one-third of the world is Christian, and out of this one-third even fewer have really caught the vision of the Man of Galilee. Thus the power available to humanity languishes for want of understanding and witness. The strange commission that Jesus left was that his followers were to tell the good news to all people. The good news is that God loves us. He is vital to our happiness and has a plan for every one of us which will insure health, happiness, and prosperity. This is the gospel (good news) that God came to earth in the person of the Son and proved to us that life can be lived in honor and dignity, and that even death can be overcome. He loved enough to give his life, and if we are to find lasting happiness and peace, we too must learn to love and give. We have failed miserably to communicate this good news to others. Instead we have sought to judge our fellows and impose our own standards of behavior, setting up dogmas and rules in an authoritarian system of religion which has manipulated and demoralized those who have felt the impact of this institutionalism. Compassion and understanding, so much a part of Jesus, seem to be sadly lacking in most of our modern church institutions and in those who claim to be his followers.

As human beings we find it difficult to understand the fact that there is a Creator who has formed us as individuals, different yet alike. Each of us is unique in talents and abilities. Some never get the opportunity to develop. Others throw away their birthright or exchange it for a mess of pottage. But each human being brought into this world is important. There was a period in history when man did not separate the secular from the sacred. Then, through a series of misconceptions, he began to think that certain events and happenings were sacred, and everyday life was secular or temporal. He began to divide himself into two entities. But man is a whole being. He has now discovered that in order to survive and attain fulfillment, he must be whole.

All life is sacred. We simply cannot divide ourselves up into parts and remain whole. A lot of disrespect for life comes from never having learned to respect ourselves. Many of us are unwilling to look at ourselves, let alone love ourselves as we have been told to do. Each human being is important, yet daily thousands are sacrificed in the slaughterhouses of materialism, greed, and injustice. Apathy continues to wear down those who care but haven't the strength to fight the battles for justice and peace any longer.

Another thing which makes me what I am has to do with my learning environment. I'm speaking of more than schooling. The experiences which I have lived through and to which I react make up a great part of my character. In his book, *I'm OK—You're OK,* Dr. Harris gives clear insights into why we react as we do in certain situations. Possibly all of us have been exposed to prejudice as a child. This develops early in childhood when the door of inquiry is shut on certain subjects by security-giving parents. The little person dares not open it for fear of parental rebuke. This goes with us through life and is difficult to change.

Dr. Harris tells us that there are three active elements in each person's makeup: parent, adult, and child. The brain functions as a recorder, putting on "tape" every experience from the time of birth (possibly even before birth).

Penfield says that whenever a normal person is paying conscious attention to something, he simultaneously is recording it in the temporal cortex of each hemisphere. The words parent, adult, and child as used here have different meanings than are usually associated with them. We are aware that there are times in our lives when we respond to the child in us, which state is produced by the playback of recorded data of events in our past involving real people and feelings. Not having the intellectual power to make decisions, a child reacts to feelings. The parent is a collection of recordings in our brain of unquestioned or imposed external events which were perceived by us in our early years—roughly the first five years of life. Everyone has a parent in that everyone is exposed to some external stimuli in the first five years of life. While these outer or external events transpire, there is another happening in the brain of the child. This is the internal happenings, the responses to what he sees and hears.

We have no vocabulary during the most critical of our early experiences, so most of our reactions are feelings. The situation of childhood produces very negative feelings, even when we have the most understanding parents (the many "no, no's" we receive help produce this). But there is a positive side, too, for we also record holding a small kitten, kicking the water, playing with the soap, nursing when we are hungry, being rocked. These are delight feelings, but the negative far outweighs them. The adult data accumulates as a result of a child's ability to find out for himself what is different about life from the "taught concept" of life in his parent and the "felt concept" of life in his child. The adult develops a thought concept of life based on data gathering and data processing. The adult is different from the parent, which is judgmental. Through the adult the child can begin to tell the difference between life as it was taught or demonstrated to him (parent), life as he wished it or felt it or fantasized (child), and life as he figures it out by himself (adult).

From the known actions of Jesus in his relationship to others we know he had matured to the point where the adult in his life evidenced itself. He wasn't bothered by the child or the parent, evidently because of his vast understanding of man which, up to now, we have lacked. He had the answer to human behavior. That answer in one word is "love." We just haven't been willing to try this way, and today modern psychiatrists and others have to devise ways to impress this fact upon us. The learning process is proving very costly. Many Christians aren't willing to learn about themselves and feel it a sacrilege to study anything other than the scriptures. Jesus accentuated the positive and refused the negative. He didn't tell us, "Don't do this or that." He did tell us to love ourselves, our neighbors, our enemies. His message was full of action words—go, do, seek, come, believe.

During the years of working with my husband in the ministry, I have always attempted to be the kind of person that most people expect a minister's wife to be. I have tried to please church members, to attend services, to labor where I wasn't particularly adept or interested— all because there was an image for me to project. But I have discovered that this is an impossible task. Furthermore, it is one imposed on me not by Jesus but by people, by the institution which I continue to love, and by the society of which I am a part.

In my awareness to determine my real self, I found that I couldn't simply act a part which I didn't feel. I have been criticized for things which I have done or didn't do, but then I also have been criticized when I did as the system said I should do.

An outstanding fact about the ministry of Jesus is that he was resolute in accomplishing the task to which he felt called. He did not allow others to deter him from fulfilling his mission in life. He, too, was criticized for his actions, but it did not cause him to forsake his mission. Thus he found fulfillment as a human being though he was, in fact, divine. He simply went about doing good. His mission was to the outcast, the poor, the misfits, and he condemned those who pretended to be something they weren't— "whited sepulchers," he called them. He opposed those who obeyed the letter of the law, forgetting the spirit. He laughed with friends, cried over the lack of understanding in people he came to serve, turned water into wine at a marriage feast, and retreated to the mountains to escape the pressures of the crowds. He invited himself into the homes of sinners and dined with them. He called simple, unschooled people to follow him, and he taught that man is a spiritual being which must be wedded into a whole person. He was about the business of human liberation. He had a consistent focus on a message of hope and redemption in the immediate future for the broken and lost—those lost to community like strayed sheep; those lost to social usefulness, like a coin kicked into a dark corner; those lost to friendship, like an alienated son in some far country.

The world today is caught up in a power struggle which robs people of their freedom and dignity. As a result mental hospitals are overrun with poor, hopeless people who can't relate their lives to any meaning or purpose.

Fear, guilt, and hate thrash around within us, superimposing a false image. John Powell says, "Most of us feel that others will not tolerate such emotional honesty in communication. We would rather defend our dishonesty on the grounds that it might hurt others; and having rationalized our phoniness into nobility, we settle for superficial relationships." It is true we don't always have to act on our emotions, but we need to be aware of them, bring them to the surface, and face them. Jesus was straightforward and honest. To the woman at the well whom he asked for a drink he said, "The man with whom you are living is not your husband." He did not condemn her, and she accepted him because of this. It was the Samaritans, the publicans, the beggars, the prostitutes to whom he brought hope. They were the people to whom the message of forgiveness was a turning point to new life. Jesus brought liberation to these people.

Because he was not judgmental, he could be honest. We haven't learned how to accept people as they are, so to cover up our feelings we walk about with a thick veneer until we scarcely know who we ourselves are, much less others.

Understanding is absolutely necessary. If no one understands me, I feel estranged. All my possessions and talents will not compensate for this feeling of separateness which brings isolation and loneliness. No doubt many a man and woman who are divorced love each other, but because of lack of understanding they cannot make marriage work. If I can be understood as a person, I can grow. In order to have a positive self-image I have to accept myself as I am, and in order to do this I need to know that God accepts me. He does not set up standards that are impossible for me to achieve, and no failure on my part will cause him to withhold his love. He does present, for my option, a pattern for the abundant life, but in no way does he condition his love on my acceptance. This is not to say that because of choices I make certain results won't follow, nor does it mean that I am content with myself or always happy with my actions. It does mean that I am loved, understood, and accepted; thus I am assisted in my growth to maturity. As one writer put it, "God has been upstairs and downstairs in the soul and knows every nook and corner. He is the only one who is in every moment of our lives co-conscious with us." There is always something held in reserve in our life that we can share with no other human being, but with God nothing is held back—nor does it need to be.

I cannot offer proof of this divine love and understanding, but because of my personal experiences with Jesus I know that God loves me as I am and concurrently that he loves every other human being. I know that Jesus loves me—not because the Bible tells me so but because while sitting alone on a windswept beach watching the waves break I felt deep within me the knowledge that there is a Creator who fashioned the universe, including every human being, because love is the very energy of life.

At the foot of my mountain I stood just as I was—fearful, doubtful, ignorant, alone. But when I discovered that Jesus was there with me and that he loved and accepted me as I was, I knew I could begin my long climb to the top to find the beauty of hope, faith, love, and knowledge. I became aware, too, that he longs for men to become united in peace and community, and that the possibility of such a kingdom coming on the earth—despite the bitterness and hate that now exist—is very real.

The first step in this peace march is to come just as you are into the arms of a loving, understanding, and compassionate Creator who knows all about you and who offers you love unlimited.

> *Spirit blazes in the dullest clay. The life of every man or woman—the heart of it—is pure and holy joy.*—Leonard

Chapter 3

IT'S REALLY AMAZING—GRACE, THAT IS!

Each person is a miniature cosmos and he is given the opportunities of committing himself and of making decisive choices. —D'Arcy

Have you ever heard someone exclaim, "If there is a God, why does he allow such misery and pain on the earth?" Or have you heard one human being looking at another who had been crawling in the gutters of life exclaim, "There but for the grace of God go I"? As a child I used to wonder what this meant. I had been taught that God loves all people. Did he then favor some over others? If there was a Being who concurrently placed heartaches and grief on the earth, mixed in a little blessing and joy, and then manipulated these at his pleasure, was this the God I desired to worship?

Grace—what a strange word. We say "grace" at mealtime. A person who has "grace" is one who is pleasing. What about the idea of God's grace being rationed out to a select few whose actions please him? Does he condemn others to the ghettos of life? If he is no respecter of persons—if all of us are in this phenomenon called life together—where does grace fit in? If God loves me just as I am, accepts me where I am, can I—by something I do—merit his grace?

One of my favorite scriptures is, "In the beginning was the Word, and the Word was with God and was of God . . . and the Word was made flesh and dwelled among men full of grace and truth." Jesus (the Word made flesh) was the epitome of grace and truth. Many names are given to the Divine Being, but to me he is the great I AM—the alpha and omega. He is God—supreme ruler of the universe. His only limitation is man's choices.

A young woman spoke very frankly to me: "Lucille, how can I believe in God when all my life everything bad has happened to me?" Divorced, with a nine-year-old son, she was finding it difficult to make a living. She had been reared in a broken home with a stepfather she felt hated her. Now, at the age of thirty, she was divorced. Problems seemed to increase daily. Although she had attended a Protestant church for two decades, she was finding it impossible to believe in God. "I want to," she exclaimed, "but I just can't!" These were tragic words, but far more tragic was the mistaken belief that God caused or allowed "everything bad" to happen to her. One of the first lessons we must learn in our climb is that God does not select subjects on whom to bestow favor or disfavor. If he did, who of us would be so presumptuous as to believe we were good enough to receive such grace?

Through the generations people have chosen their own willful way. Perhaps it is true that the sins of the fathers are visited on the children. Because of these wrong choices, evil has progressed in the world. People have literally willed themselves into this position, because they have been unable to seek the ways of truth and light, choosing instead to follow their own desires. Scriptures accepted by Judeo-Christians tell us that man stands condemned because he sees light and refuses it, but "to as many as believed, power was given."

No person ever approaches death without knowing, even while refusing to admit it, that there is a glory and vastness beyond the mundane everyday life most of us live which is charged with power and light. This energy and creativity is what life is all about. Sometimes we find this out very late and then have few years with which to test the newfound strength. People have been living under the law so long they scarcely can comprehend the love which motivates creativeness and life. They must be free to become. They need freedom from self-will which produces wrong choices; conversely this freedom will bring fulfillment and peace.

While there must be form and order to life, religionists have become so bogged down with dogmas and institutionalism that many have failed to witness to the majesty and power of God and Christ. Jesus is the man with the Plan, and that Plan spells success and purpose for those who connect with it.

At the time Moses gave the Ten Commandments, which consisted of a long list of "thou shalts" and "thou shalt nots" (mostly nots) men were not ready for a greater law. God gave the people what they could live with. If he had said to the Israelites, "Come unto me for I am meek and lowly of heart," half of them would have turned to the cult of Baal, seeking revenge on their enemies. So he told them, "Love God, honor him, honor your parents, do not steal, do not commit adultery, do not lie, do not covet, etc."

God was limited therefore by men's understanding, and it was by their own choice that they lived under the law. With the dawning of the new era, when the promised Messiah appeared and God came to earth in the person of his Son, this law was to have been fulfilled. Yet today people continue to live under this rigid law—they still believe in "an eye for an eye" and are unable to respond to the greater law, "Love your enemies. Do good to them that misuse you."

Christ came to show us how to live and die by the law of love. Rather than being victims, we can become victors as did he. How glibly Christians through the ages have sung, prayed, and spoken about this love of God, yet all the while remaining attached to the strict law. One who truly loves will never hurt or destroy another. There have been men in every dispensation who have seen clearly the path of love and where the potential could lead. Most of us have not been willing to let self go in order to be able to love; thus we suffer the results. It is out of our own choosing that we continue to endure frustration, for the law of love promises relief from such turmoil. This does not, by any means, exempt us from suffering; through suffering we grow. It does, however, mean the ability to accept whatever life offers and, by God's grace, the chance to become victorious.

Because we continue to hug our woes to ourselves and moan about our lot, we lack purpose; we literally starve the creative nature which is our birthright.

Jesus brought a workable plan by which any person can live provided he is willing to pay the price. The discipline comes high, however. Surrender of self-will has always been the deterrent. It is so very difficult to satisfy the ego.

There are many pseudoreligionists in the world, just as there are pseudoacademicians who seek to cure the ills of life through gaining more and more knowledge. Although education is necessary, one seldom learns to love by going to school. While the mind is involved in study, the heart must also learn to respond through living what is learned. Too often compassion and love are withheld from the learning experience. I have been associated with social workers who attained the highest degree in their field yet failed miserably to communicate love and goodwill, and this failure showed plainly in their daily lives.

Some religionists make Christianity so complex and full of speculative theory that the experience of love which the heart must have to survive is exploded by the so-called authoritarianism of many institutions. Such an organization, while claiming to represent Him, retains the right to cast from it those who "sin and

49

transgress the law." Christ, by his own admission, came to the sin sick and the unrighteous. On one occasion he said, "Those that are whole need no physician." His mission, like that of his church, is the reconciliation of man. Yet most churches have set themselves up as judge and jury. By such overt action they have alienated those who are most in need of help. God's grace is for all men—even those who have refused life and simply roll over and play dead.

Jesus came to prove to us that life can be lived in love, that death is not the end, and that we can overcome whatever obstacles we encounter. Our attitudes determine what we become—physically as well as mentally. One young woman who works with me discovered she had cancer in the beginning stages. She was sent to the hospital for radium packs, then cobalt treatments for six weeks. Although these treatments made most people ill, she suffered no discomfort of any kind and was always cheerful. Her physician remarked that he had never seen anyone like her. Her secret was the knowledge that she was in the hands of a loving God, and she faced the future unafraid.

Just to know that such power exists in the universe, that there is Someone who loves me so much that he was willing to die for me, forces me to acknowledge that I must not spend my life in hopelessness. Life is to be celebrated!

The common denominator of life is love. Yet there is really only one way we can understand, to any degree at all, the depth of the love God has for man—that is to love another human being and be filled with so much compassion that we would gladly bear the burden of his sin and release him to all the joy his soul can hold.

A minister related to me in a moving way an experience he had with a friend. He loved this man very much, but his friend was under condemnation because of his own choices. He was faced with great heartache and pain because of the burden life had placed on him. The minister recalled, "I wanted more than anything to be able to take that man's burden on myself, to bear it for him and release him from it." Have you ever met someone who because of wrong choices had brought the pressures of life down around him? How did you react? Judgmental? This is law. Compassionate? This is love. It is relatively simple to help those who are considered worthy. It is love-motivated understanding that causes us to help those who, through willful actions, have made a mess of their lives. If the truth is known, no one deserves God's grace, but it is poured out alike on all.

When I have seen my children weighted down with the sins and ills of this world, I have longed to share their burdens—to free them to the joy I know awaits them when, through right choices, they receive an enlarged vision of life and its true mission.

The following story is true. I personally share a deep bond of friendship with the family. It is an exceptional testimony of what the power of prayer and love can do, and of how much worth each individual really is. Here it is in my friend's own words:

The hospital was quiet that icy night in March 1972 as I lay in the five-bed ward unable to sleep. There was no significant physical pain keeping me awake, but the brittle sound of sleet against the dark windows caused me to shiver as I wondered if our middle daughter was warm and dry . . . or even alive. She had left home with a girl friend the day after Christmas, and we hadn't heard from her since. This had been her third runaway attempt in the year and a half since she'd become entangled in what we were later to find was drug abuse.

I felt I had prayed every conceivable prayer up to that date, but this particular night I was finally able to say, "Father, apparently we have been unable to reach our daughter in a way to which she could respond. Please come to her aid now wherever she is and cause her to make contact with people who can communicate with her and help her, even if it be that they take our own place in her life as parents."

We spent the following eighteen months condemning ourselves and studying everything we could pertinent to the drug scene and the problems of youth today. During the summer months that followed my husband's and my emotions ran the gamut from anxiety and depression to frustration and hate. Then it began to occur to me that while I loved this girl as a daughter, I was not loving her as a person. There was a growing awareness that until I learned to put aside the disgust and disdain I felt over her actions and began to love her as she was—a child of God—that she would not be returned to us.

By the end of June I began to long for the day that I could put my arm around her and tell her how much I loved her and wanted to understand her hurts.

The phone call came the last week in August. A tearful, frightened girl of seventeen was calling from Virginia asking, "Mom, can I come home?" Could she come home! We could scarcely wait for the next day when we could pick her up in Detroit. During the drive back she poured out a tragic tale of her experiences, particularly of one desolate night when she had reached bottom. She had no place to go, no money, nothing to eat. It was then that a young man found her and took her home to his parents for help. This happened one cold rainy night in the middle of March, 1972!

Last Christmas we shared an evening with this family. The girl described in the story was a changed person. She embraced me warmly and said, "It's so good to see you." She had been liberated because someone cared enough to respond to her, and because her parents learned to love an alienated and lost child. She was a recipient of God's grace because of another human being's love.

What would happen if each of us could feel another individual's pain? In the science fiction *Childhood's End,* Arthur C. Clarke envisions a time when the Overlords come down to earth and prepare it for the next stage in human evolution. Before this can happen the world must be reformed and improved. Such cruelties as bullfighting, for instance, must be ended. The people are warned to stop this sport, but they refuse. The next Sunday a spaceship appears over the biggest bullring in Madrid. When the first pic is thrust into the bull's shoulder, a piercing scream rises from the audience, for the Overlords have caused each person there to feel the pain just as the bull feels it. There is no more bullfighting.

What would be the result if each of us could share the feelings of all humanity at the same time and with full force? I'm sure there would be a terrible, agonizing scream heard round the globe. (Because of the pain we have experienced, we do know how others feel, but we bury this feeling somewhere in our consciousness. The world weeps for words unspoken, for confrontations postponed, for moments squandered, for beauty overlooked, for loving compassion denied, for judgment rendered, for indifference.) But following the screams, joy would return—the joy of existence and recognition of the simple fact that life is to be lived each moment of every precious day despite the pain.

While we are limited in bearing the pain and frustration of another, we can share with understanding and love the grace of God as we seek those with whom we come in contact.

How can anyone believe that God stoops to man's law of retribution and retaliation? Isn't it true that the rain falls on the just and the unjust? Then regardless of what occurs to us, it doesn't matter. What is important is our attitude toward it—which, in turn, determines our ability to overcome.

We were not created to crawl like worms—to sink into the pit of debauchery. We were created to enjoy life, to run and not be weary, to have a productive life filled with creative impulses allowed to mature. Jesus told a group of followers, "The kingdom is already come among you." It is here waiting for us to unlock the door—but we hold the key!

While we need order and institutions, they are merely the means to the end—not the end. We must be free to respond, to expand horizons, to fly to the heights of excellence. We must not be cast into a mold. Every person is different. We must be free to march to our particular drumbeat without building up a storehouse of guilt because our way may be different. We are not puppets on a string. We have been created with abilities to co-create with God as we survey the wonders of this earth and indeed the entire universe.

Whenever I become unhappy with a position, I do all I can to improve it, then I turn the matter over to God, praying that a way will be opened for me to serve in some other capacity. I have yet to experience failure to receive an answer. Doors have been opened in marvelous ways. Grace reaches down to me and answers my needs.

It's really amazing—this grace of God—and it is open to everyone who seeks the crystal mountain.

You are a child of the universe, no less than the trees and the stars. You have a right to be here and whether or not it is clear to you, no doubt the universe is unfolding as it should. —Desiderata.

Chapter 4

WHEN THE COOKIE CRUMBLES

Suffering and trouble belong to life. To abstract [them] from life would mean stripping life of its form and shape. Only under the hammer blows of fate, in the white heat of suffering, does life gain shape and form. Therefore the destiny a person suffers has a twofold meaning: to be shaped where possible and to be endured where necessary. —Victor Frankel

Most people know that Job was a man who suffered all the "slings and arrows of outrageous fortune" and remained faithful. Many, however, are not aware of Job's doubts and misgivings. At one point his wife said, "Job, why don't you curse God and die?" His reply still rings through the ages: "I know that my Redeemer liveth, and though the skin worms destroy this body, yet in my flesh shall I see God."

Job had everything the world could offer— money, possessions, family, health. As the story goes, the devil approached God and said, "Sure, Job is a good man. Look at all you've given him.

You have built a hedge around him and I can't get through." So God allowed the adversary to get through to Job. But he failed. At the end of Job's trial—we are told—he was better than at the beginning. All that he lost was restored to him. This story sounds as if God bestowed a life of happiness on Job because the adversary had been unable to lure him away. I maintain, however, that God doesn't select certain men on which to bestow favors. I believe Job's good fortune was the result of his own actions. In the final analysis, whether this side of the grave or not, we all have the ability to create our own heaven or hell by the choices we make. Job decided to take what life offered him, good or bad, and use it to the glory of God. Could this be the secret of the abundant life—not that we escape suffering but that we are able to overcome it?

It all depends on our attitude toward life and our purpose for living. A young boy had an unfortunate experience and ran crying into the house. Just then his father tooted the horn and asked him if he would like to go for a ride. The boy turned to his mother and said, "Just wipe my tears away. I'll finish crying when I get back." The mature person has this quality. "I'll cry later, but just now I have work to do!"

I joined hundreds of others who were peering at the top of a twelve-story building where a lone figure perched precariously. On the sidewalk below, firemen and policemen were running back and forth with a net. On the same level as the distraught woman, a minister and policeman were trying to talk her down. "Have the net removed," she said, "or I'll jump right now." They complied. "Won't you come in and talk this over?" they asked her. She shook her head and suddenly without the signal for which all were watching, she plunged to her death below. Those nearest the spot where she fell turned away sick with the sight. One young man near me put his hand to his mouth, visibly nauseated. Others stood stunned as the body was removed. Later her story revealed that she couldn't cope with the strain of life. She felt that no one understood her.

All of us experience confrontations, conflicts, and crises, but these are what make life challenging. Some conflicts, of course, are more penetrating than others. But when a real crisis arises, there is an inner strength on which we can draw if we have prepared in advance.

A man standing on the beach one day found himself next to a little boy about four years old. The conversation went this way.

Man: Why is the sea salty?

Boy: Because the sailors are always crying because they are always going away.

Man: Why do people cry when they're sad?

Boy: Because the windows of their eyes must be cleaned so they can see better.

The understanding of children often amazes us. Their perception is so valid.

Perhaps there is no relationship in the world today in which more conflicts arise than between husband and wife, parents and children. It is as difficult to arrive at mutual understanding between members of a family as between nations. Some are strong. Some are weak. The strong find it difficult to understand or cope with the weak. They set up standards and expect others to fit into the mold. Each person is an individual and has his own mold.

The ringing of the phone cut through the stillness of the early morning. My husband answered it and as I heard him respond to someone at the other end, I realized that a couple had just about reached their limits of endurance. After hours of arguing, they had decided to call him. He extracted a promise from them that they would cease speaking to each other, go to bed, and he would be over in the morning to talk with them. He spent several hours the next day with them. While not revealing who they were, or their particular problem, he told me what advice he gave. "I said that they would have to compromise in order to come to a consensus and resolve their problems." At times, life is a compromise. In most every argument between husband and wife, there are apparent causes—conflicting ideas, opinions, ideals, and taste—but behind these are the real ones: lack of love, touchiness, fear, jealousy, self-centeredness, impurity, sexual incompatibility, and lack of sincerity. All people have differences of opinion, but this isn't bad, in itself. However, wisdom does not come by polling ignorances or joining viewpoints but by baptizing honest differences in a higher light. Man desperately needs a higher intelligence than his own. Through association with Jesus, he can find the stability needed for those times when the human element gets beyond his ability to help.

A woman executive of a Girl Scout Council told me that many people wondered why she didn't have ulcers. "It's simple," she said. "I do the very best I can; then I let my Partner take over. God does for me what I can't do." She was a deeply religious Catholic woman who took God's word literally.

61

Most people, however, do not radiate joy and confidence. Take a walk down a busy street and look at the faces around you. Can you see a grim determination which says, "Let's get on with this business of living and get done with it"? We are so prone to ignore each dawn as the glorious opportunity for another day of life, and we have somehow lost the ability to shake off our stress and fear of yesterday so that we can face a new beginning. Of course, there are days when all the cookies crumble, but no problem lasts forever.

The secret of health and happiness lies in successful adjustments to ever changing world conditions as well as to the daily stresses of mere existence. There is a great difference between psychological and chronological age. One person may be much closer to the grave at forty than another at sixty. True, age depends largely on the rate of wear and tear or the speed of self-consumption, for life is a process which gradually spends the given amount of adaptation energy that we inherit from our parents. The human body, like tires on a car, wears longest when it wears evenly. The two great limiting factors which are set, once we are born, are our supply of adaptation energy which we inherit and the wear and tear that the weakest vital part of our body can tolerate.

Once we are born—unless we kill ourselves—we must complete our time on earth. We can do much through choice to get as far as possible with our given body structure, a natural supply of energy, and certain social conditions. We can live and express our personality at a tempo and in a manner best suited to our inherited talents. The real fuel of life is not the food we eat but our adaptability. The ability to accept what happens to us, either through our own choices or because of our inability to control situations, will determine our actions. If we are unable to accept life with all its conflicts, then most likely, if pressed severely enough, we will resort to suicide. Not all people who take their lives are psychotic. There have been times when I have seriously thought of escaping the pressure of the daily grind, but deep in my reservoir of memory is my relationship with Christ. I have never cried out for his help that I have been denied. My experiences have proved to me that there is great power in prayer and meditation. A noted scientist has said that prayer is the greatest energy in the universe. Prayer and love and God are all linked together. We cannot separate them, and when we choose to house divinity in our lives we can be guided, molded, and sustained regardless of what is brought to bear against us. The story of Job is the epitome of faith in a divine Presence.

At times we may feel that we are about to break under the burden of life; still we can rejoice because of the life present. Nothing that happens to us can defeat us unless we allow it to do so. We are not alone in the world. The sooner we discover that there are others like us who have the same hurts and disappointments, the richer we shall be.

We are in the world like a bee in a hive, and so I must not shirk its burdens or turn my back on it. If I face reality and am faithful in playing my part, I shall encounter other persons like myself and meet them as persons. A dialog will ensue and the world will become more and more open and I enlist my faith in it.—D'Arcy

A mature person lives by encountering reality, meeting it head on, and committing himself. Friedrich von Hugel says we need the spur of risk and adventure to keep us from falling asleep. Tension depends on a motive and re-sistances. A falcon cannot ride the air without resistance—its hurl and gliding rebuffs the wind. This is true of a plane also.

On the cross Jesus cried out, "My God, why have you forsaken me?" Contrary to what some theologians say about this being the opening lines of the twenty-second Psalm with which

Jesus was familiar, I believe he actually felt forsaken at that moment. For most of us, the presence of God in our lives is not something we live with daily; the times are few and far between, though they certainly don't have to be. When we are aware of God's presence in our lives, these become meaningful, unusual times for us. His absence is more the normal experience for most people. But for Jesus, it was the other way around. For him the normal thing was to feel the presence of God, the Father. This experience of his absence was conspicuous because it was so unusual.

Except for his plea on the cross, Jesus addressed God as **Abba.** This is what every Jewish boy called his earthly father. It was the most intimate address anyone could use, and no one ever thought of addressing the Most High God as such. There are no easy answers to what happened on the cross, but one thing is certain. Those words Jesus uttered speak to us today in a strangely poignant way, for all of us have at times felt completely alone. We look about us at the world and feel certain God has forsaken it.

Life has never been without discipline and pain, both personal and social. For some there are times when the world is beautiful because everything is right; then suddenly they receive one blow after another. Perhaps they feel as young Baron von Hugel did when he was eighteen. After his father died, he developed typhoid fever which left him deaf; then he suffered a prolonged nervous breakdown. The young baron—normally so buoyant, radiant, and optimistic—wrote: "The world which, until then, had looked so brilliant to me, turned out so distant, cold and shallow."

There is beauty in the world, but in many cases it has been displaced by ugliness. There is goodness in the world, but there is so much violence that it seems goodness cannot long endure. There are people who manipulate, dehumanize, and misuse others. There are those in high places who, because of an inner compulsion to "play God," deface and humiliate their fellowmen. To one suffering such a sting, retribution is the first emotion to arise. But the power lies in loving our enemies . . . in turning the other cheek and doing good for evil. Human beings have never been willing to practice this except in isolated situations and not for very long at a time.

In my own life I have discovered great power in being able to turn the other cheek. If I can just get past my wounded pride, my hurt self, and pray for the person who has abused or misused me, I can receive great strength for my life.

The Cross tells us that Jesus shared our humanity in experiencing all the hurt and pain that we do. His friends betrayed him, his beloved disciple denied him, and they all ran out on him. He was alone, and he felt his aloneness. But the historical empty tomb validates the option that Jesus became victor, proving that he was never really alone.

It isn't sacrilegious to feel at times something of the desolation of the Christ who said, "My God, why have you forsaken me?" Such moods may well be phases of our earthliness. But to be trapped in such a mood is another matter. Occasionally I have found myself in a position completely beyond my control. I couldn't see any possible way out. Wherever I looked, there were walls and curtains and barriers—or so it seemed to me at the time. What I couldn't control, others could and did. They shared their light with me, and it was more than enough to enable me to be a light to still others. It is a reciprocal agreement, for when light is created in darkness, darkness is no longer the problem. Jesus came to be the light of the world, and I believe he is the light in every man.

There will always be the little foxes that pick

at us—those small annoyances that produce tension and wear us down. In addition to these there are major burdens. In my life, one such event occurred ten years ago.

We were returning from our vacation in Florida to our home in Ohio. There were six of us in the car, including our two children (Carol and John), and my husband's sister and her husband. We had enjoyed our trip greatly. It was about five o'clock in the evening and raining. Lee had turned on the lights since it was dusk, and because of the roads being slick we had slowed to around forty-five miles an hour. Carol, who was fifteen, and I were in the front seat with Lee. I don't know what happened because I was dozing, but I am told that another car suddenly swerved into our lane of traffic. Apparently the driver did not see us or thought he could get around and back in line. At any rate, there was only a brief second for Lee to turn the wheel a hard right. As the two cars met, we received a glancing blow, a hard one, but the slight turning of the wheel prevented a complete head-on collision. Then a series of peculiar things happened. Our gas tank flew off down the road. Carol went through the front windshield and back again. I received a broken arm and concussion. Two ambulances were in the line of traffic, and a hospital administrator also, who immediately returned to his hospital to prepare for us. A nurse in one of the ambulances rendered first aid to Carol who might have bled to death without her help. John, our son, had a broken leg. Katie and Haynes had broken bones but none that couldn't be repaired. Lee received a broken collarbone but was able to handle everything before he collapsed. Probably the most spectacular occurrence was the fact that two physicians who had never before asked to change their shift had done so that day. The two replacements happened to be an orthopedic surgeon and a plastic surgeon—just the kinds of doctors we needed. We all recuperated, though I was in a coma for two weeks and there was some doubt that I would survive. Carol had plastic surgery three times; today the scars are barely visible. John's leg healed so perfectly that when he was examined for the Air Force, the doctors could not detect the break. Later he told us that when his dad was praying for him, due to his intense suffering, the pain suddenly left, and he felt two hands molding his leg together. The plastic surgeon who repaired Carol's face remarked each morning, "Someone has been working on you at night." He was amazed at the healing which was taking place.

Long after the accident someone asked me, "Why did God allow such a thing to happen to you when you were doing his work?" My answer was, "Why not?" I don't think God allowed it to happen. A man chose to use his judgment which resulted in faulty driving, but God was there on the scene and blessed us beyond measure, proving again to me that with faith all things are indeed possible.

Regardless of what happens to me, I am aware that I am in the hands of a loving Creator. I use my intelligence to its limits, then allow him to take over. I am assured he will supply my every need. I'll be able to endure whatever happens, regardless of how many cookies crumble. I just have to be willing to sweep up the crumbs and start another batch.

Anxiety is inevitable in this age of crisis. Don't make it worse by deceiving yourself and acting as if you were immune to all inner trepidations. God does not ask you not to feel anxiety but to trust in him no matter how you feel. Faith is a part of the mystery of life. Einstein has said, "The fairest thing we can experience is the mysterious. It is the fundamental emotion which stands at the cradle of true art and science. He who knows it not can no longer wonder, no longer feel amazement, [can no longer have faith] is as good as dead, a snuffed out candle."

Earth's crammed with heaven and every common bush afire with God; only he who sees takes off his shoes—the rest sit around and pick blackberries. —Browning

Chapter 5

FREEDOM TO BECOME

What we must reach for is a conception of perpetual self-discovery, perpetual reshaping to realize one's best self, to be the person one could be. — John Gardner

"How do you feel about the bill in the Senate regarding mandatory fluoride in our water system?" I asked the women in my office. The bill was in the process of circumventing the voters of Oregon.

"I'm not sure," one remarked. "I think it should be a personal choice, whether or not we want this in our water. This way, it is being forced on us."

Members of the Supreme Court of the United States have decreed that should a woman so choose, she can have a legal abortion. They stipulated that this was a personal choice between a woman and her physician, citing the fact that the use of illegal abortions had resulted in the death of more people than the ruling they were making would. Is this a matter of personal choice?

We're told that eventually it will be against

72

the law not to wear seat belts in our cars. We must limit our speed; motorcycle enthusiasts must wear helmets; etc. What is freedom? Do we possess it? Is it society's duty to protect us from ourselves, or is there a better way in which we can find freedom to respond to ourselves, to God, and to others?

Recently we built a house. Permits ran into the dozens. While we owned the property we were restricted as to what we could or could not build, even down to how many windows a room should have. A multitude of restrictions bound us to the kind of house we could build.

Tons of paper work have become necessary for us to run our governments, communities, churches, social services, schools, and even our private lives. Is it possible we have become so involved with papers that we have forgotten we are persons? Is 1984 already here?

Today people are used and manipulated, while things are sought and loved. Tillich says, "The first thing I want to point to is the absolute character of the moral imperative. . . . Its source is the encounter of person with person, an encounter in which each person constitutes an absolute limit for the other. Each person, being a person, makes the demand not to be used as a means."

It is true that certain events beyond our control determine our history. We enter this life without choice in the matter of parents or environment. Further we inherit certain tendencies due to our parental background. We enter the stream of time without any known wish on our part to be here. The culture and mores of poverty or deprivation can brand us for life. There is no absolute freedom.

Flying at 33,000 feet above fleecy clouds I felt an urge to jump out and walk on them. But I was not free to do so. It would have meant instant death. Actually only a bird is "free as a bird," and a bird cannot swim like a salmon or run like a dog. Each must live within its limits.

We, too, must live within our nature. However, there is a freedom inherent in all of us which is determined by our personal choices. Social mores—rules laid down by someone long ago—determine our freedom. I am not free to walk up to another person and slap him without paying the consequences of such an act. Neither am I free to go out into the streets nude without paying a penalty. Society has rules and regulations against such behavior. But within limitations, all of us have a certain amount of freedom to be, to become, to fulfill potential, and to respond to life with joy and hope.

Man is here for the sake of other men; above all, for those upon whose smile and well-being our own happiness depends and also for the countless unknown souls with whose fate we are connected by a bond of sympathy. Many times a day I realize how much my own outer and inner life is built upon the labors of my fellowmen, both living and dead, and how earnestly I must exert myself in order to give in return for as much as I have received.—Einstein

The United States was founded by men who knew that the world around them was largely hostile to the idea of freedom, and through the ages this freedom has had to be proved worthy of survival. In order to secure true freedom, there must be choice—the right and ability together with the responsibility of choosing wisely and well—yet freedom without destiny is a vacuum. No man, I repeat, escapes the responsibility and mystery of choice.

There are times when we would like to retreat to a remote seashore or mountaintop to escape the daily duties that demand so much. Life does place a burden upon us, yet to refuse to take our part in living is perhaps the one great sin which puts us in chains of our own making.

Some of our statesmen tell us that America may survive if enough people care. The foes of freedom are still ready to argue that sloth and self-indulgence make a free society simply impractical. The world is full of people who believe that men need masters.

Our institutions often present chains which bind us in many respects—our schools, our communities, and even our churches. There is rigid social stratification. We are required to submit to certain beliefs in order to escape the responsibilities of freedom. This results in a sense of uselessness, which is one of the most severe forms of psychic deprivation. Thomas Huxley has said that this is the greatest shock our system can sustain. One has only to look at the senior citizens of today and see the hopelessness in their eyes because they no longer feel of worth.

Jesus told his followers that the truth would free them. What did he mean? Over and over we ask ourselves, "What is truth?" We believe that we need goals in order to find happiness and freedom. (And happiness isn't all sweetness and light—it is striving toward meaningful goals, despite burdens and problems.)

To find such goals requires motivation and discipline, for real freedom means discipline and response to truth regardless of where we find it. We are a long way from understanding the complexities of individual motivation. There are times in my own life when I simply can't whip up enough discipline and energy to do what I know I should, even though I want to. The matter of will is involved. We don't know why, but from early life some people seem firm in their goal patterns while others are tossed about by events like a ball on a ping-pong table.

We are all bound by fear. "The most powerful resistance resides deep in each of us. We fear to relinquish our neuroses, our discontents, our diseases. We fear any significant personal movement toward that which would save us and our world" (Leonard in *Transformation*).

Fear reacts on the endocrine glands causing dysfunction of the whole system. Psychologists tell us we are born with two fears—fear of falling and fear of loud noises. By maturity, however, we have accumulated dozens of fears. Heading the list is fear of our own thoughts. We deny certain thoughts and feelings. This denial is "ego protection," and this "ego protection" can keep a person a prisoner within the realm of his own mind.

Fear is a presymptomatic warning. It is the motivating power behind all repressions and suppressions. The need is to bring fears, commonly called "anxiety neuroses," into the light and face them. If this can be done, they can be overcome.

John Dollard, psychologist at Yale, has listed seven kinds of common fears: fear of failure, sex, self-defense, trusting others, thinking, speaking, being alone.

Fear of failure. This comes of thinking that one is inferior, small, or weak. It causes some not to try at all, others to give up easily. All people have such feelings at sometime and obviously when they do, they are defeated before they begin.

Fear of sex. So much indoctrination has led to fear or misunderstanding of everything having to do with sex that damaging feelings of guilt have resulted. A large number of married people are actually afraid of sex and do not take advantage of their freedom to cement their relationship within the framework of this natural and normal expression of love. Enlightenment is often only intellectual; emotionally there is still a deep-seated mistrust and a clumsiness in dealing with it. Despite all the publicity, the how-to books, the X-rated movies, etc., sex remains one of the biggest hangups of the age.

Fear of self-defense. This stems from a loss of self-respect and results in the failure to defend one's own rights and insist on a fair share of things. Many people suffer in silence. Meekness and humility as Jesus taught do not deny the right to be children of God, and this entitles people to a place of their own.

Fear of trusting others. This is a repeated flaw in human relations. People often feel that if they want something done they must do it themselves. Perhaps they once trusted others who didn't measure up.

Fear of thinking and speaking. This is based mostly on the education of the conscious which causes so many inhibitions. Children are punished for whispering in school, and they grow up fearing that some undesirable word or thought may escape or betray them. They are afraid to be themselves, because they are afraid they won't be accepted as they are.

Fear of being alone. One of the most common fears, this makes restless, anxious individuals. They cannot meditate or even direct their own thinking in silence. The TV or stereo must be playing. They are fearful of being alone with themselves, yet ultimately this is where all must end up. People have to live with themselves, not only in this life but for eternity. No one ever escapes from himself. No one knows for sure what lies beyond this life or, as Hamlet put it, "For in that sleep of death, who knows what dreams may come?"

Recognition and admission is the beginning of self-honesty and a subsequent solution to freedom. Fear drains the body of needed energy and causes many psychosomatic illnesses. Jesus has told us that, with him, we can do all things. I have found this to be true in my life. When I reach my limitations, when doubt and fear plague me, I simply say to him, "It's your ball game now." I've yet to fail to get help. With each assistance, I enlarge my growing edge a little so that the next time I can go a bit farther before I reach my limits.

Another thing from which we need liberation is guilt. There is a normal guilt which we all feel at "wrongdoing," depending on our idea of what this means. But there is a much deeper level of guilt which is the stepsister to normal conscience. One is destructive, the other constructive.

When we "hold things in" they go down to the nonverbal level where they fester. This results in all kinds of psychosomatic diseases and mental illnesses. We need to realize that each of us is unique. We all hear different drummers and must be free to follow the music which we hear (provided it doesn't injure another). The concept of freedom does not lie in surrounding ourselves with luxuries. Though we may often be tense, worried, fatigued, if we are free and truly dedicated we shall be ever pursuing goals. Some of them may be unattainable, but we'll keep on trying anyway.

We are just beginning to understand that free people must be their own taskmasters and set their own goals. A free person looks upon life not as a burden but as a mission. He is here to accomplish something.

Like life itself, freedom needs many sources of nutrients to sustain it. It is not something that can be obtained once and then passively held on to. The difficult struggle must be endured by each new generation. What Thomas Paine taught us on the eve of the revolution remains true today: "Those who expect to reap the blessings of freedom must, like men, undergo the fatigue supporting it." This is as true of freedom of the self as of a nation.

There is another freedom which is also important—freedom to respond to others. In order to be able to see the true worth of all people, we need the ability to see them as through the eyes of God. Leaders in churches and other benevolent organizations can send emissaries throughout the world repeating over and over again the familiar clichés that "all people are of great worth" yet at the same time treat those of their own household with hostility. We view with indifference those with whom we associate and sit in judgment on others because we have not been able to realize our own worth.

The fifties and sixties are known as the ages of anxiety. The decade of the seventies, we are told, is the age of depression—of wondering what it's all for, where it will all end. Mental illness is fast approaching the number one problem in the health field. A few years ago the statistic was that mental illness would strike one in five families. Today, it is predicted that it will hit every family to one degree or another. Suicide is the leading cause of death in the age bracket of fifteen to twenty-five. Once every minute someone tries to kill himself, and every twenty-four minutes someone succeeds. It is the fourth major killer of adults and moving up the ladder fast. We must ask ourselves how much involvement we should undertake to prevent a person's cutting short his life. If people are of ultimate worth, what about our response? And are we free enough within ourselves to respond?

In viewing others through the eyes of divinity we can never pass judgment. We simply can't know their heartaches, hurts, and pain. All we see is what they do, but God sees inside them and knows what is happening there. We need to become aware enough to develop at least a degree of this compassion and not react or condemn another person because of his outward action.

More specifically, freedom to respond means that—black, red, yellow, or white—each man must be of enduring worth during his lifetime. He must be allowed to climb his mountain in his own way. He must be able to develop without being overcome by a set of rules and standards.

Laws are needed now, because without them there would be chaos, but there will dawn a day when we will understand what Augustine meant. When we have learned through the discipline of freedom, the love of brotherhood, respect for each other as human beings, nothing we shall do or say will hurt or destroy another or defame God's universe as we have so grotesquely done at this point in time.

Freedom to respond is our being able to care about one another not because we are of the same religious persuasion, belong to the same political party, are of the same race or national origin, or are in the same tax bracket. It's being able to respond and care because we are all human beings sharing a space on this planet for a few wonderful years. It's caring and knowing we are cared about.

During the period of time I worked with the Girl Scouts in Portland I developed a friendship with an orthodox Jewish woman. Sixty-four years of age, she had more vitality than I did. A widow, she wanted to be extremely independent of her children and wanted to continue work until she was sixty-five. After I'd been on the job only a few months, I was home one day with the flu. I'd been under extreme pressure during the Easter season, moving into an unfinished house, beginning a new job, and having my husband away for a week. Frances told me the day I returned to work, "I woke up this morning at 2:30 and started to call you." Startled, I asked her why. "Because I knew your husband was away, and I was afraid you had no transportation, and you might not have enough food in the house and no way to get any." This is caring! I was interested in her religious background and discovered that we shared a mutual love for God, the Father of all.

If we search deeply enough we'll discover that though we differ in religious and political views and social status, we have much more in common than we have differences. We are all creatures of the universe with innate longings and desires. We are all seeking to belong to something or someone, and we seek in frustration until we find this freedom to respond to the Creator, to ourselves, and to others.

Being free to respond makes us vulnerable, and this subjects us to pain. But this is part of life.

We need to be free not just to be but to become. As free people we see ourselves as liked, wanted, accepted, lovable. Because we feel this way about ourselves, we feel this way about others also.

Jesus said that the person is worth more than the system—worth more than the rules and regulations. Self-assertion must come before self-denial. Parents who put the brakes on their adolescent children confuse these two movements. There is a period when parents have full responsibility to mold and guide their offspring. For proper growth and development children must be allowed to become individuals—real people.

While shopping one day my husband and I spied two preschool youngsters sitting in chairs waiting for their mother. Both spoke to us very shyly—"Hi"—and smiled. We responded and carried on a conversation for a few minutes. As we turned to leave my husband remarked, "They're just like people, aren't they?" Of course what he meant was that they were just like big people with the need for companionship and love, but there are too many who look on children as nonpeople. They are not toys. The early love or indifference which surrounds the child determines to a large degree the maturity level he reaches. All adults share this responsibility whether they are parents or not.

I feel we are all responsible for each other. Until we grow in awareness of the sense of divinity housed in each human being, regardless of his actions, our vision will remain clouded.

I had been in my new position with the Girl Scouts only a short while when I found it necessary to hire another employee. After interviewing some twenty people I narrowed the applicants down to two. One was a black WIN (Work Incentive program) trainee, twenty-six years old with three children—one, five, and seven. I knew that Cynthia was a person who desperately needed the position and who would prove beneficial to the organization. Being a WIN trainee, she received half of her salary for twenty-six weeks from the government; this enabled me to hire the other person also. Cynthia has proved capable beyond my wildest hopes. She is a joy to be around. She is eager, a fast learner, dependable, conscientious, and determined to make good.

Israel—a Mexican militant with whom I shared a week at camp—came to the United States to find out all he could that would help alleviate the suffering of his people. Born a Catholic, he renounced his church because he felt it had failed to help the poor of his country. During the week at our church family camp he heard many things about the kingdom of God coming to fruition on the earth and he was deeply impressed with the plan. While he still considered himself an unbeliever in God or any formal religion, because of events which transpired during that week and the Spirit which was present, we shared a common idea of love and peace for all peoples. At the last service Israel said that he was going home to Mexico and try to put into practice this love and peace that he had heard about. He said he knew beyond any doubt that such a kingdom of peace would one day exist on the earth. We felt a kinship to this man which went beyond beliefs or cultures.

Many people do not like life. Their early training has left them with a built-in recording which says, "Live prohibited." But I say, "Live it to the fullest." We renounce too many things of which we know little. We have a tendency to localize evil outside ourselves. In former years this resulted in witch hunts. People were afraid of that which they didn't understand. For example I find many people fear the Book of Mormon without ever looking inside its pages to discover that it is a history of the Americas, doesn't contradict the Bible and is for those who accept it another witness that Jesus came to the earth to show men how to live.

Through the years there have been many who have discovered their crystal mountain through association with divinity. The Old Testament prophets looked for the coming of a Messiah. Abraham, Moses, Jeremiah, Isaiah all spoke about a Deliverer—one who would break their chains of bondage. What the people failed to understand was that bondage could be inside a person, and freedom did not necessarily mean the breaking of literal chains. Freedom begins inside the person who realizes his own worth, his purpose in life, the reality of attaining a goal, and the ability to move toward that fulfillment.

Perhaps there will always be those little foxes that spoil the vine—people who misuse us and cause us to forget momentarily the divine Presence which is an innate part of every human being. But even these people can prove helpful to us in our climb. It is easy to love those who reciprocate. There is rapport between some we meet in our daily contact with life. At times words aren't even necessary. A smile, a look, a firm handshake, a pat on the shoulder all stroke us in a positive manner. We meet less frequently with those with whom we can be "soul brothers" where time and age prove no barrier.

From the point of view of the holy, we do not belong to ourselves but to that from which we come and to which we return—the eternal ground of everything that is. This is the ultimate reason for the sacredness of the person and consequently, for the unconditional character of the moral command not to destroy our essential being which is given to us and which we may disregard and destroy.—Tillich in *Search for Absolutes*.

Truth is absolute, but our knowledge of it is not. We grow day by day, experience by experience, learning a little truth here, a little there, and as we learn, we discover how much more we have yet to learn. Still this seeking takes us up the mountain and grants us the freedom to respond more fully.

To be nobody-but-yourself in a world which is doing its best night and day, to make you everybody else—means to fight the hardest battle which any human being can fight; and never stop fighting.—E. E. Cummings

Chapter 6

CALL TO EXCELLENCE

For those who are willing to overcome fear and learn through pain, there is delight of high adventure in store, travels of the spirit, festivals of accomplishment in realms now hidden from our senses. — Leonard

Without question we are living in strange times. For many of us, the world has turned topsy-turvy. Long-standing values have been torn asunder. Venerated beliefs have fallen by the way. Traditional social and political practices and convictions have become casualties of a new time, a new age, a new way of thinking. What is real? What foundation is "shatterproof"? Upon what changeless star can we set our fix and guide our lives?

These are some of the questions which face us as we confront life in a changing world. Among the basic corollaries of change are pain, anxiety, and uncertainty. We see this uneasiness manifested in all walks of life—marital tension and stress, the generation gap, the intense pain which comes from grappling with questions of existence. New and increased tensions are being placed on every social unit—family, community, government, industry, and church. These systems affect us, our families, our neighbors, our world.

This is also a time of alienation. A once prevailing sense of the supportive community has diminished. People—increasing at a steady pace—appear only as faces in a lonely crowd. Today individuals are frantically searching to be understood, to be heard, to be treated as persons with dignity. They are asking, "In times of crisis and stress who cares enough to listen, meaningfully and compassionately?"

In this world, filled with inequality, injustice, and war, can the call to excellence be relevant? Does it really matter if what we do is our very best . . . or is it enough to just get by? A cursory look at workmanship in any field would indicate that craftsmanship is vanishing. When faced with purchasing anything—furniture, clothes, equipment, labor—we notice that few people seem to take pride in accomplishment any more. To many, it is simply a job they want to finish as soon as possible, collect the fee, and go on to another inferior task.

In places where we have been assigned over the years, I have been appalled at the lack of pride evidenced in home construction. Joy in the accomplishment of a job well done and the feeling of fulfillment which comes with it seem to be disappearing as technology and machines take over many tasks.

Work has become a dirty word in some circles. True, work was made for man, not man for work, but work implies goals and intimately affects the person performing it. Perhaps no labor alone can enrich the person; yet labor, regardless of what it is, when done in the most excellent manner brings a sense of accomplishment nothing else can.

There are many varieties of excellence. In science there is the excellence that leads to new ideas, new theories, new creations. Some people find their greatest expression in teaching or research. Others excel in art, music, in human relations. There are even those rare beings who excel in being parents.

We live in a competitive society. This involves comparisons between those who are great in their field and those who are not. The excellence we are most concerned with, however, has to do with filling our own individual potential, living life to the best of our ability, with our own special limitations, regardless of the lack or hindrances which may be placed in our paths.

A lot of excuses float around for not doing

things well. We are all in a hurry, flying off to someplace, to do something, and completing the vicious circle day after day. Seldom do we take time to be human, much less to do our jobs in an excellent manner. The clock and calendar are potential killers of excellence. I have worked among people who were always rushing to get the job done. This was due partly to surrounding pressures and partly to the attitude of "it doesn't really matter as long as the job gets done." I'm not speaking of being perfectionists. We are all human and make mistakes. What I have in mind is "living on tiptoe" and accomplishing the goal that will result in personal fulfillment.

We need goals for which to strive. The hopelessness and aimless wandering which exist today among the masses need to be replaced by a life-style which gives purpose and meaning to daily living. Thousands never realize such fulfillment. Poverty and ignorance keep them from experiencing such realization. The necessary stimulus to growth and achievement is lost in the struggle for survival.

Yet many who have the proper environment for such growth and motivation fall into a rut and cease growing. They lose their awareness and become apathetic, drifting from day to day in meaningless wanderings. Perhaps this will always be so. No doubt there will be those who will waste their talents and dissipate their resources. But unless enough people care to respond to the call to excellence, such waste on a massive scale may well eventuate in the demise of our society.

The person who answers this call realizes that he cannot dedicate his life to small purposes. He does not strive to amass things to feed his vanity, but he does do his best to become one who is esteemed. This is a wish to be, not merely to appear to be. Excellence is that quality beyond success. One may be successful in the eyes of the world without touching true excellence, for excellence is in the person and is not conferred by the office he holds or the wealth he commands.

Excellence is a thing in itself, embracing many kinds of achievements at many levels. Happiness lies in the active exercises of a man's vital powers along the lines of excellence in a life affording scope for development. One must, of course, be competent, but excellence arises above this.

Jesus told his followers: "Be ye perfect even as God is perfect," but this perfection has to do with a quality of life—what is within a person, his motivations, his understanding of his fellows—and is not connected in any way with a long list of "thou shalt nots."

In America we mass produce almost everything—quickly. But we cannot mass produce character in an instant—or in a lifetime—because this is a matter of personal identity and growth. Shakespeare puts it this way: "To thine own self be true, and it must follow as the night the day, thou canst not then be false to any man."

We need causes to believe in. We respond to causes because in so doing something better is brought out in us. Our lives take on new meaning. Every institution in this country should be in the business of developing individuals to their greatest potential. Instead most of them manipulate people, use them, move them about like pawns on a chessboard. The church, along with the schools, community, and government, comes under this condemnation. If, however, we believe what we profess—that the worth of the individual is great—then the idea of individual fulfillment within a framework of moral purpose must become our deepest concern.

There are standards to be met in every calling. Every honest calling has its own elite, based on excellence of performance. This comes from acquired skills but also from what a person is.

The person of quality will delight in what he does, whether it is building a birdhouse, writing a novel, or planning a business transaction. He is impelled by his principles to do well the job that is his. This implies a fundamental integrity; the workman know what he is doing and carefully brings his skill and personality to bear on the task.

It isn't enough to be against error and ignorance; one must offer his own potential to discover this excellence and truth. Such a person lifts his head above the crowd to see a horizon fitting his abilities.

In the book, *Jonathan Livingston Seagull,* a moving story is told about a gull who, daring to be different, soared to excellence, even though he was banished from the flock. He dared to fly higher, to explore farther, and discovered a more excellent way to freedom. But when he returned to tell his friends about his newfound freedom, they could not understand. Instead, the elders banished Jonathan from the flock. Banishment was not the sorrow of his life; the thing that caused him to grieve was that those to whom he tried to teach the better way wouldn't even listen. They were content to lead mediocre lives.

There is a price to pay for learning the

discipline of excellence. If we discover the joy of the more excellent way—the secret of all flights that await us—then we must be prepared to pay the price. We will discover, as did Jonathan, that each level of understanding promises greater excellence and that we grow in awareness, going on to perfection through our own choices. Failure to do this means we fix ourselves in an immovable position to which we are forever bound.

If we select a cause, we need to make sure that the ultimate value of it will offset the inevitable discomfort and trouble that go with accomplishing anything worthwhile. In order to be able to do this, we need to develop a sense of values of things.

How do we achieve this more excellent way? How can we gain the motivation needed to stimulate us to want to achieve a standard of excellence in all we do and in what we are? What forces precipitate the feeling, "What's the use?" or "Why not give up"? Why are people so lethargic when technology has reached a zenith and men have walked on the moon?

Most of us realize that education is not limited by a few years spent in school. Education is a lifelong process. This means that we must keep in mind the attributes needed to survive errors, to keep walking on a road that seems to be without end, to rise above disappointments and heartaches, to lie awake at night pondering over broken hopes and frustrated plans and a future that at times may be wholly dark, then to arise in the morning and go about the business of the day with renewed determination. It is to keep on keeping on.

Excellence demands self-control. Nothing will protect us from eternal pressures so much as control of ourselves, based on ideals formulated within us. Excellence calls for enthusiasm. Enthusiasm provides the perseverance that overcomes impediments both real and imaginary. We need to keep on trying to overcome resistance to change, for we live in a changing world, and we must measure its pulse each day.

For me, there is only one way to achieve such self-control and enthusiasm—that is the way laid out by Jesus. People draw inspiration from different sources—home, school, church, community. Experience can be a harsh teacher, but it is effective. My experience with the Christ helps me correct the errors in my life—whether in thinking or in doing.

We are born into this world to offer something of ourselves to it. Unless we do so, life may seem meaningless. The person who does a slovenly job—whether janitor or judge—lowers the tone of society. Yet excellence implies more than competence. It implies a striving for the highest standards in every phase of life. We must be our own taskmasters, set our own goals, achieve our own excellence. It cannot be forced on us.

And what if striving all our life does not bring the excellence we desire? There is a certain satisfaction in trying, even if we do not have total success. As Robert Browning put it in Rabbi Ben Ezra, "What I aspired to be and was not comforts me." Chiang, the old gull, told Jonathan, "Heaven is not a place, nor a time. Heaven is being perfect." Could it be that heaven is attaining excellence in whatever we do by growing and growing and growing some more? Jonathan learned from the elder gull that perfection doesn't have limits. We keep going on. The trick to perfection is to first stop seeing ourselves as limited, as trapped inside limited bodies. From there we go on to perfection to learn about love—for love, as spoken of by Jesus, is the embodiment of excellence.

Most of us are still shackled by fear and doubt. We need to emerge into the sunlight of faith and joy and know that we are more than flesh and bones. We have within our being the possibility of attaining not only excellence but eternal love.

The call to excellence remains clear, and those who are free to respond will hear, be aware, and answer it.

Human fullness is self-actualization. The inference is that until we reach out to be the thing for which we were created, our socialization is the socialization of a robot and not a human.

The robot may program himself to the culture and get along socially, but is not a human being until he actuates his own capabilities quite uniquely and apart from anything society can teach him. —A. H. Maslow

Chapter 7

BIRTHDAY TO A NEW LIFE

A civilization that denies death ends by denying life.—Paz

"Are you just going to live out here by yourself and die?" the newscaster asked the old man. "Yep," he replied rolling tobacco in a cigarette paper. "I'm just going back where I come from—out there in space—and continue to live, just like I was born all over again." This was part of a story about an old prospector in the hills of Montana who was living alone in a shack, mining for gold . . . and finding it.

When asked about death Helen Keller replied, "I know there is something more beyond the grave, because at eighty I am just beginning to learn to live." She faced the thrilling prospect of a sight-filled existence—something she had not experienced in this life.

Although it is inevitable, there is hardly any event for which we are less prepared than death. We fear it because we fear the unknown. Someone has said that this motivating fear of death lies behind all our fears and prevents our living life to its fullest.

Eric Fromm reminds us that we tend simply to deny death and with it one fundamental aspect of life:

As is always the case with repression, by being removed from sight the repressed elements do not cease to exist. Thus the fear of death lives an illegitimate existence among us. It remains alive in spite of the attempt to deny it, but being repressed it remains sterile.—*Escape from Freedom.*

The early Christians faced death with joy. Thrown into the lions' den, crucified, tortured in various ways, they amazed those who stood by watching because they sang, even while suffering. But these Christians had a viable witness that there was something beyond death—something they didn't quite understand, but they knew it was there just the same, and it opened doors which brought freedom and peace. It was an adventure to which they looked forward.

At least twice in my life I have held hands with death—once when giving birth to my first child and ten years ago as a result of an automobile accident. While recovering from this accident, I had an experience which defies description. I cannot put into words how I felt, but as I lay in a coma for two weeks, I had a remarkable encounter with divinity. Because I was not responding to the drugs given me, the doctors felt I was dying. I had no wish to return to this life, but I survived. Perhaps, as it has been said, "There is a time to live and a time to die. . . ." At any rate, I know now that the worthwhileness of living is at stake in the manner and thoroughness with which we meet the issue of death. Inseparably bound up with the worth of living is the estimation of our own worth.

I hold no fear of death. My personal belief is that life goes on in another dimension where I shall continue growing to greater potential than I have dreamed of in this life.

I hate the so-called Christian funeral of today, where death makes mockery of life. Someone has said that funerals are for the living, not the dead. In this instance, it may depend on our viewpoint and our ability to face the issue squarely prior to the time we must confront it.

I feel the time has come not for radical action but for systematic stocktaking and exploration of the nature of the problem of death in all its ramifications. If we are to be successful in "climbing the mountain" we must review in our

103

minds how we feel about death—our own and that of our relatives and friends. We must make plans for this adventure in life.

The disposal of the body at death has a long history—from the mummies of ancient Egypt to the newest method of freezing the remains. We know that the Egyptians embalmed with a refined process which modern man has failed to match. According to a team of experts at Wayne State University in Michigan, a recent autopsy performed on a 2,600-year-old mummy turned up a perfectly preserved heart.

It's amazing how ignorant most of us are as to what procedures to follow when someone in our household dies. First a physician should be called. If none is available, a call to the county medical investigator or coroner is in order. If death was brought about by suicide, accident, or some other unnatural cause the police must also be informed (this would bring a medical examiner). The physician or medical investigator prepares a health certificate indicating cause of death. This form requires certain statistical facts relating to the deceased—age, sex, date of birth, social security number, parents' names, etc. When this has been done, the body may be removed to the funeral home.

In most states if a body is disposed of within

twenty-four hours embalming is not necessary. However, if a person died of any communicable disease the body cannot be transported without embalming.

The unstable dollar and staggering prices of all commodities should make us aware that the cost of "leaving" is not going to get any less. Thomas Mann once said, "A man's dying is more the survivor's affair than his own." If this is true, costs are very significant. It would be considerate of us to make as complete arrangements for our burial as we can rather than leave it to survivors who may be grief-stricken and unable to clearly define procedures.

It is generally considered that four separate categories of charges make up the cost of a funeral: (1) those which specifically involve the funeral director, his professional services, the use of facilities and equipment, the casket and vault sold by him; (2) charges dealing with the disposal of the body, the grave plot, opening and closing the grave, or cremation with an urn and columbarium fee; (3) a monument or marker for the grave or niche; and (4) miscellaneous expenses such as flowers, newspaper notices, limousines, burial clothing, and out-of-town transportation of the body.

The foundation of the traditional funeral is

the embalming process which, together with the fact that bodies usually are kept four or five days rather than being buried within a twenty-four-hour period required by law, necessitates a decision. Embalming has a long history, but not as it is done today in the United States. True, the practice of preserving dead bodies with chemicals, decorating with paint, powder, etc., has its origin in antiquity—but not in Judaeo-Christian antiquity. This incongruous behavior toward the human dead originated with the Egyptians and reached its high point in the second millennium B.C. Thereafter, embalming suffered a decline from which it did not recover until it was made part of the standard funeral service in twentieth-century America. Early Christians regarded embalming as a pagan custom. Mummification of the dead in Egypt was gradually abandoned after a large part of the population was converted to Christianity. We know from biblical history that Christ was bathed, wrapped in a linen cloth, and placed in the tomb.

Some contend that it is therapeutic to the bereaved to have "public viewing of the body." Their argument is that if we don't look upon our loved ones in an open casket we just can't be sure they are really dead. Professor Volkart of

Stanford University states that he knows of no evidence to support this view. John Kennedy and Dwight Eisenhower were not in open caskets for public viewing, yet who would deny that both of these men are dead?

The Roman Catholic Church requires that the following instructions be observed: the body be decently laid out, lights placed beside the casket, a cross laid upon the breast or hands folded in the form of a cross, the body sprinkled with holy water and incense, and burial in consecrated ground (suicides cannot be a part of the latter).

The Jewish religion specifically prohibits display in connection with funerals. There is no embalming, and burial takes place within the twenty-four-hour limit. The wooden coffin is loosely constructed, unadorned, and no flowers may be placed inside or outside. All show and display of wealth is discouraged. Moreover the Rabbi is responsible for arrangements for burial. In Israel today uncoffined burial is the rule, and the deceased returns to the earth in a simple shroud.

Early Christians used white as the symbol of death. Today, black is the traditional color. Yet many Protestant denominations are striving to get their people to hold memorials in the church after simple graveside services. In Colonial America, those of the immediate family bathed and prepared the body after death, wrapped it in a sheet, and buried it in a wooden coffin.

Death is a mystery, but we have made it a chamber of horrors. And that is something it is not! We can help those we leave behind by preparing a letter of instructions; this eliminates uncertainty and confusion when death occurs, for it enables survivors to handle the affairs and other specifics in an orderly manner. A close estimate of a traditional funeral today in the United States is approximately $2000, depending on the part of the country and the options selected. (There *are* options, and one should be aware of them.) More people are requesting no flowers, asking instead that contributions be made to a favorite charity.

I believe there is no cessation of life even though the breath goes out of the earthly body. I feel life continues in a new and broader dimension—one not bound by time or the afflictions that prey upon the physical body. I cannot conceive of a Creator seeing his creation cease in such a dismal manner. I think that part of the reason Christ came to the earth was to let us know that death is not the victor, not the end. Many so-called Christians act as if it were, however. I have attended funerals where emotional hysteria became so intense that people had to be forceably taken away from the coffin. To me, this reeks of guilt, not love and devotion.

Many people resist any attempts at death education because it has such emotional impact. Death cannot be "taught," but perhaps it is possible to clear away obstacles in order to achieve a better understanding of this encounter which all must face.

What happens at death won't make any real difference, for the miracle of a resurrection will be just that—a miracle!

> *We who must die demand a miracle.*
> *How could the Eternal do a temporal act,*
> *The Infinite become a finite fact?*
> *Nothing can save us that is possible.*
> *We who must die demand a miracle.*
> —W. H. Auden

Chapter 8

BRIDGE TO HOME

And after all the journeying, all the pain and joy, we may discover that the transformation was difficult to grasp, not because it was so far away but because it was so very near. To find the immense world of delight is, in the end, to come home again, where it always was. —Leonard

In Aldous Huxley's *Brave New World* social scientists plot our course and physiologists tell us what we'll look like. But there still seems to be no overall direction. Theodore Gill has said:

We have studied our poor, paradoxical, chaotic society, analyzed it, graphed it, put it down on charts and missed the point completely. . . . We have made of life a bridge without ends; a laughable thing that starts nowhere and doesn't go anywhere and does nothing in between.

In the familiar musical, *West Side Story,* we listen to a poignant affirmation in the song which had deep meaning for Maria and her lover. "There's a place for us—somewhere, a place for us." This, then, becomes the cry of all human beings. Life is expressed in the mythology of places. We all need somewhere to be.

Psychiatrists point out that the child who has been able to grow up in a wholesome, love-filled home will find a welcome everywhere and will have the security of knowing he has somewhere to be. When the family is such that the child cannot fit himself into it properly, he spends his life looking everywhere for other places and becomes an unceasing wanderer. Most human excesses—alcoholism, drug abuse, sexual aberrations—result from this never being able to find somewhere to be.

All of us are looking for God, whether we realize it or not, for he is the bridge to home. Some never call him by name, but they are desperately seeking a system of unlimited support. People have limits. We look for absolute faithfulness in a person, but because we are human, there are elements of faithlessness in us all. So we seek for someone who can never be at fault, regardless of what happens. This universal desire for support is quite natural, since we are the most vulnerable of living creatures and the only ones who recognize our frailty. Thus we seek a plan of security.

Children will often call to one another, "Save me a place in line." All of us are constantly looking for our place, wanting assurance that we belong, striving for the fulfillment so necessary to self-identity. This can be summed up in one word: community—somewhere to be. To discover this we need to find the bridge to home.

Life is not an abstraction. To exist is to occupy a particular space to which we have a right. This is why it is so important for us to form our own identity and project our individual image. Today this need often goes unfilled in favor of the masses into which we allow ourselves to be herded.

We are told by physicians that all of us long for the feeling of being secure, surrounded, and protected as if by a mother's arms. It is perhaps a vague remembrance of our intrauterine life before we were born. This need for total protection is none other than the need for God. This is true of those who believe in him . . . and even in those who claim not to. The unbeliever's faith is revealed in an untiring search for real support and his rebellion when those on whom he has been counting betray him. God does not, however, reserve his support only for the believer. Jesus taught that all people, regardless of their conduct, are to receive this support without discrimination. God's patience is inexhaustible. The more personal experiences I have and the more I hear of the experiences of others, the more I wonder at the unimaginable patience of God.

Most of us are aware of human hostility toward life. This appears to become more overt each day in interpersonal relationships. Philosophers, poets, artists, and theologians have wrestled, as Job did, with the inequities which life seems to lay on us.

Tolstoy said, "One can only live when one is drunk with life. As soon as the drunkenness fades, one sees that life is nothing more than a fraud, a stupid fraud."

Yeats wrote, "Life is a long preparation for something that never happens."

Do we actually believe that life will end with a whine and a whimper?

It does little good to pretend that as human beings we have the natural capacity to celebrate life as a beautiful adventure, lived unselfishly from start to finish. For some people the thought of death is not the ultimate irony. Rather there is the feeling that this comes out of being little or nothing—the feeling of being cheated—which results in more hostility.

Did Jesus experience such hostility? Could his weeping over Jerusalem have been an expression not only of love and sorrow but also of hostility against "the way the ball bounces"?

Dr. Paul Tillich has said:

Even in those who have completely surrendered to life, our hostility towards life is manifested in cynicism and disgust, in bitterness and accusations against life. We feel rejected, not so much because of life's objective darkness and threats but because of our estrangement from its power and meaning. He who is reunited with God, the Creative Ground of life, the power of life in everything that lives, is reunited with life. He feels accepted by it and he can love it.

We need to agree that life accepts us. There is a section of life which is nearer to us than any other and often the most estranged from us— other human beings. We are all aware of those hidden regions of the soul in which things look quite different from the way they appear on the surface. In these places we can find hidden hostilities against those we love. Often we love without being sure of an answering response from another. When we are open and free, we become vulnerable to such pain. Certainly it is not amiss to see the human Jesus suffering under the same pressures which bear upon us. He had a deep need for his life to be strongly directed toward unification with his friends, unity with his father, and the healing of all people as members of one family. Surely this is the core of life—the bridge to home.

If we can feel accepted, then we can ultimately accept ourselves, and this means forgiving ourselves. Many go through life guilt-ridden because of deep-seated feelings and emotions which they cannot express.

The ruthless competition which deprives people of a feeling of security makes many of them sick—not only those who are unsuccessful but also those who are most successful. We have fought victoriously against many forms of physical illness. We have discovered drugs which cure with almost miraculous power. But many people cannot stand this health. They need sickness as a refuge into which they can escape from the harshness of an insecure life.

It is Jesus who challenges individuals and nations to be healed. This presents difficulty. The nations know that becoming healthy means becoming whole and united. This can be expanded into the realms of politics, economics, social justice, and religion. To be whole we must forsake the need to be ill. Can we then receive the healing power in the projection of Jesus who is called Savior? This can be answered only by those who have experienced this healing power. No one lives in such a state all the time, but there are moments of grace in which they participate in perfect wholeness—the wholeness of God being in all.

Healing, then, is born out of hostility, out of our affirmation about that which pesters and festers and makes us angry. Healing within us grows as we are able to say "yes" to life, "yes" to the joys and sorrows that make up living, and "yes" to God, the Ground of our being.

The choice remains in our keeping. Even Jesus said that his life was not taken from him; he laid it down of his own free will. The responsibility for our choices also remains in our keeping, and we must be willing to bear the burden of such decisions.

We are not only seeking a place for ourselves but a place where we can localize God, for we need someone to worship. Perhaps the great problem of our age is that we attempt to place God in one specific place with one select people. He cannot be localized. He is universal. We cannot pin him down to one spot or one event.

In their early wanderings, the children of Israel wanted to isolate God. They needed something visible with which to identify divinity, so God provided the Ark of the Covenant which they carried with them in their travels. Today, however, those who experience the Holy

Spirit in their lives realize that God is universal—at work everywhere in the world. We need no "holy of holies" with a veil separating God from us. We need him to walk beside us. The sanctuary can be anywhere the love and compassion of Christ appears to minister to the needs of humanity. A pulpit, a building, an altar made of wood and stone cannot be holy as such. Only compassionate action initiated at such an altar makes it sacred.

Christ selected the seashore, the mountains, or the shade of a fig tree to bring his concern for and appeal to those he desired to reach with ministry. His place was wherever he found persons in need. There he offered his love and forgiveness.

Most of us relegate God to the sanctuary, when in truth he is everywhere. Because we are unable to comprehend the immensity of such a Being, we try to make him fit our limited mold. The idea has resulted in our placing too much emphasis on the church and not enough on the person-God encounter. It is true that we must reconcile our need both for this universal God and for a personal Savior. God *is* personal. He does select places in which to reveal himself. He breaks into history and enters into dialogue with men at particular times and locations. Biblical history is replete with such examples. While he is interested in the entire universe, he is also concerned about each individual. So far, however, we have been unable to fathom this depth of concern. Our values, therefore, are confused and our society is in trouble.

There are numerous stories in the Old Testament that tell of God's effecting a personal confrontation in order to bring forth a universal message. Moses beheld the burning bush which was not consumed. Jacob wrestled all night with an angel. Abraham was willing to sacrifice his only son because he thought God commanded him to do so. Such confrontation today would doubtlessly drive away most believers. Yet the faith of Abraham led him to be a father to his people. God spoke to a young man in a grove in order to bring forth a universal message—the message that God lives and speaks to men today. This message has changed the Christian world.

We need to remember that the contents of such events are far more important than the places where they occurred. Too often we have tried to fit God into our churches while denying his presence in the world. Yet God's purpose is the salvation of the world—not merely of the human race but of all creation which must be freed from bondage and restored.

Jesus found it necessary to have a place of his own. He was bound, as are we, to places. A manger in a stable in Bethlehem was selected as his place of birth. His mission, though universal, was accomplished in events, in personal encounters, in clearly defined places which led right up to Calvary and the tomb.

Although I haven't stayed in one place too long in my life, I believe I have discovered the bridge to home. The day has long since passed into oblivion when the average person lives in one house or in the same town all his life. The old family homestead has given way to superhighways on which members of the family travel great distances in separate directions. We are a mobile society. As a result, interpersonal relationships have suffered. Insecurity may come as a result of our mobility. Once we were nourished by roots which went deep into the past, but no longer. There actually is no one place most of us can call our own. This desire for roots goes far beyond a house or city. It really has to do with belonging, with fulfillment, with the security of accomplishment, and of feeling wanted. Many new life-styles have been born with the forceps of change, and change is always painful.

As I've already said, my favorite spot is near

the beautiful waters of the Gulf of Mexico where white beaches stretch for miles. Yet much as I love it, I realize I must learn to be content in other places. After living in Kentucky (my birthplace), Florida, Ohio, and Michigan, I now call Portland, Oregon, home. Yet somehow I still feel at times like a visitor, like a wanderer in this great Northwest.

Personally, it's hard for me to move from place to place, adopting such as my own for a time, then moving on. No doubt as one gets older there comes an innate longing for the security of one spot to call "home." Perhaps it can be described as an inner ache that never really goes away. Can there be such a place, or is there more to our desire to cross this bridge to home, this "somewhere to be"?

We loved our years in Florida, but we can never go back to those exact times. I have learned, however, that I can re-create beautiful feelings. It has to do with what happens inside me. After his moving experience, Jacob said, "Bethel I'll raise." He desired to build an altar to God and promised to return. In fact, he raised many altars but probably never returned to that exact spot. Bethels can be raised anywhere we choose.

On one occasion Jesus told his followers, "I'm

going to prepare a place for you, so you can come and be with me." Did he mean heaven (somewhere "out there") as we've been led to believe, or is it possible that a place of eternal verities will be prepared for us here in this world? Could this be the new earth we hear about? Will there be that ultimate place somewhere that fills all human yearning? Is the ultimate longing of man for this bridge, and can it be found in this life?

If so, we know that the earth must be transformed and renewed. The process isn't always clear, but we are aware that it can come when we learn to love enough, when we become vitally concerned about every human being we encounter and desire for him the same place we desire for ourselves. When this happens, we are near the peak of the crystal mountain.

Perhaps the place we all seek is not only a place but a condition of being. The type of faith which moved Abraham is not easy to achieve. It carries with it a price—possible frustration and disappointment and heartache—yet isn't this the goal to which we have committed our lives?

I believe that God is everywhere. I've seen him in the twinkling lights of the city, and in the stars as I've flown 40,000 feet above the earth. I believe he must surely walk the streets where

121

affluence and poverty pass each other without so much as a nod, on the battlefields where men kill and are killed, in the prisons where empty-eyed people count and recount the days. I'm convinced God is in all the sordidness and misery of life, but most of us shun this picture of him. We prefer to keep him caged up in the sanctuary with its stained glass windows and organ music. If I find my place with him trying to help alleviate suffering, what about my own frustrations?

There are times when I cry, "Let this cup pass," and times when, like Jonah, I want to run away and hide. But these pass and once again, through growth and grace, I am able to find a place of my own which has nothing to do with houses or cities. It is then that I become willing to leave it and journey into far countries. In so doing I need to form instant friendships. Time will not allow for long associations.

Can we learn to have meaningful interpersonal relationships in this mobile society? Jesus left his home and traveled for three years forming ties that lasted through death and beyond. It was the quality of ministry he gave—the personality he shared momentarily—which proved to have such a tremendous effect on those around him. Some of my most valued friends are those I have shared the least amount of time with. By the same token, I also have friends that I have known for twenty years or longer who are not bound by distance or age.

We all have a desperate need to see the bridge to home—to have a place of our own before we can move on. We need to receive before we can give. Most assuredly we cannot give what we do not have. Perhaps our roots actually lie in the struggle and anguish of our lives and those around us as we endeavor to make something meaningful of our brief existence on this earth. One thing is certain. We never find our place alone. It must involve other travelers. As we climb our mountain we'll meet others. Together we need to be willing to move out to new frontiers in order to reach new peaks.

If our lives would be harmonious, we must demand unity of place. Our spiritual pilgrimage involves our total lives and depends on our wholeness. Wholeness comes through right relationships with divinity and the rest of the human family. One is not possible without the other. Only when we have achieved this can we find our place and the bridge to home.

There is a place for all of us. When we reach it, we'll know it. And love will be there. It will lead us to the bridge where fulfillment of our deepest longings will flood our souls with peace.

We shall not cease from exploration and the end of all our exploring will be to arrive where we started and know the place for the first time. —T. S. Eliot

Chapter 9

THE IMPOSSIBLE DREAM

The future is beyond knowing, but the present is beyond belief. We make so much noise with technology that we cannot discover that the stargate is in our foreheads. But the time has come; the revelation has already occurred ... the guardian seers have seen the lightning strike the darkness we call reality. And now we sleep in the brief interval between the lightning and the thunder. —I. Thompson, *At the Edge of History.*

As a nation we are in deep trouble—in our domestic life and in our foreign relationships. Watergate has pushed to the forefront the very distrust which has threatened the freedom we so prize. We may try to hide from this, to close our eyes and ears, to refuse to hear the cries of distress. But even those of us who are most comfortable, most protected, have an uneasy feeling that all is not well. We are aware that we do not live in a community, nation, or world of trust, of mutuality, of understanding and caring.

We know that we do not live as the Creator intended us to live.

We must be aware that this age with all its marvelous technology and potential is also a time of great loneliness. We cannot communicate with each other. We are separated by a great gulf which widens with each dawn. We are separated by race, by religion, by culture, by age, by apathy, and by ignorance.

Yet in the midst of all this, something good is happening. The impulse for freedom was never more alive than it is now. The terrible problems of our lives are now out in the open, and because we are aware of them we are in a position to do something positive about them.

This is a frightening but hope-filled time, for God is at work in our world. If our blindness can be shattered so that we can understand and respond and participate in that which is being created we can fulfill our purpose individually as well as collectively.

The ideal of the kingdom of God coming on the earth with all its inherent justice and opportunity has been called by some the impossible dream. What a wonderful challenge and what a terrible and awesome privilege is given to us to open doors, to provide experiences that can change lives—but only if we care enough to use the very best methods, set goals, and work toward them, allowing nothing to deter us.

In order to effect this, we need to learn to listen to others, even to those with whom we disagree. To remain open and aware we need to use our intelligence to understand what is happening in education, government, community, and church. We need to listen to the youth, to see the cause behind the symptoms of their rebellion, and we need desperately to dethrone self.

We are separated from the mystery, the depth and the greatness of our existence. We hear the Voice of that Depth, but our ears are closed. We feel that something radical, total and unconditioned is demanded of us, but we rebel against it, try to escape its urgency and will not accept its promise.—Tillich

Thus, if we are not part of the solution, we become part of the problem.

We cannot patch up our world like a torn balloon. Wholeness must be brought about by each individual's commitment to the dream and to the fulfillment of that reality.

Perhaps racism is the most critical problem we face today. This will vanish only when the revelation of responsibility and awareness penetrates enough minds. Responsible people face two alternatives. One is to love and continue to

127

live. The other is to hate and die. The choice remains ours.

If we choose love, we must be prepared for action. If we do nothing, we are choosing the alternative of death. We have the power to change our vision, to act and thereby to change the world. To allow life to leak out, to wear away by the mere passage of time, to withhold giving and spending it is to choose nothing. Harvey Cox has said, "Not to decide is to decide."

The time has come for a revolution of the constructive, the positive. There is need for leaders, initiators, and educators—people who are committed to be motivators and facilitators to make the dream a reality.

Martin Luther King told his followers, "I have a dream!" For him, it was the impossible dream, at least during his life on earth. Yet who knows in which dimension he may now continue his struggle for this dream? Through centuries men have dreamed of a society of peace and brotherhood as a way of life, sustained and nurtured by love, compassion, and understanding, coupled with mutual respect for all life.

Since the beginning of recorded history, men have searched for this dream. Abraham went out looking for it. Yet today this city still awaits the building made possible by those committed to love and peace. The followers of Abraham have established a nation, and they too continue the struggle for the dream with difficulty.

In an interview, Golda Meir remarked that the saddest part of her life was in finding that the people of the Jewish nation were not one in their dream of brotherhood. Will the division that has always plagued mankind continue, or is there a way to gain unity even through diversity?

Eons ago God presented man with the dream, but man wanted more, so through his own choice he opened the door to life and walked into the vast world where fear, doubt, and adversity awaited. Perhaps the dream will remain impossible until enough are willing to walk back through that door to their Creator's side and follow his will for their lives.

I feel that the major deterrent to fulfilling the dream is man's insatiable desire to be his own god. Instead of exercising control over himself through discipline, he has sought control and mastery of others, thus preventing the society of free people living together in mutual respect and peace. Idols come in varied forms, but placing self at the center of the universe is the one act which causes man to play God.

In the rock opera by Rice, *Jesus Christ Superstar,* Jesus sings a poignant song to those who would make him an earthly king and give him power and glory: "Neither you Simon, or . . . or . . . understand what power is, understand what glory is, understand at all." Man has failed miserably to understand what real power and glory are. Power comes in many earthly forms—money, success, achievement in the top echelons of career, community, or government; but very few have glimpsed the real power and glory which could be theirs if they would but place God at the center of their universe. When death comes, no earthly power is of any help, and the glory of existence is more often than not neglected as weeds cover tombstones.

The life of Christ revealed that real power lies in loving, in giving, in nurturing, and in understanding the purpose of life which includes death. Man's ultimate glory will be to live in the presence of the Creator for which he was made.

Without hopes and aspirations, we would be little more than the animals that roam our planet. They too have intelligence, can be trained to obey commands, and possess devotion for their masters. But animals never worry about debts or dying. Neither do they hope and dream of a better world.

Achieving this new society will not mean that the rich will divide all their earthly possessions with the poor. Abundance is not a curse, or is poverty a blessing. It will mean, however, that there will be no poor, for all men shall have their needs and just wants satisfied. This condition does not imply a welfare state; it will not come through force or by enforcement of governmental law—rather it will be the result of love and compassion. There will be a well defined system of civic, social, community, and government planning aimed at integrating the whole man. There will be work. The city of peace will not be an idle place. Masses will not be forced to stand in line for food stamps or subsistence checks. Dignity will be restored. But for those unable to work—the old, the sick, the handicapped, the children—there will be a place where they can feel useful, and their needs will be met. The arts will bloom and, as the poet expressed it, "a mightier music fill the sky." This wholesome society will not be a communistic state where people are subservient. The state will exist to serve man, not the reverse. Revolutions are born out of deep-seated hungers within the soul, but often when the revolution is over those who fought so hard for their rights deny others these same rights.

It is true that the world today is in turmoil. Peace is not won easily, if at all. Yet as far removed as this seems, transformation is dawning. Apathy is the greatest hindrance to the realization of the impossible dream. We sit watching television, viewing the atrocities which happen around our globe. Sometimes we are stirred to write our senators or congressmen; more often we just feel sad for a few moments, then dismiss it from our minds. But in our deep consciousness the injustice, inequality, and brutality gnaw at us, causing what Leonard called "dis-ease"—and, in many cases, actual illnesses.

If we are aware of what life is all about—if we are aware that the earth is being smothered with tons of concrete—then we'll become awakened to the need to preserve land in its natural beauty, to plan where possible and refuse to allow industry to grow bigger, suffocating the green earth.

Technology does not have to ruin our natural environment. We have demanded more and better appliances to create a life of ease—but ease for what? Foul air that we can't breathe? Water that we can't drink? Do we control technology, or does it control us?

If we care enough we can awaken in time to the awareness of the transformation which will end this desecration of the earth. This is the ease which has become our dis-ease. The source of energy from which all life stems is in distress.

To merely survive we must have fresh air and pure water, regardless of how well industry does or doesn't function. We may have to start all over again at the bottom of our crystal mountain, but if we are willing to achieve the dream, we can attain the heights and find the joy of reality in just such a kingdom of peace and plenty.

If each of us is willing to learn—through pain, if necessary—to relinquish our failures and discontents, to face reality as it is, and then to move out to change our environment, the impossible dream can move into focus.

We need the awareness that we all depend on each other, not only for food and water but for that oneness without which we are not whole persons. This is the magic planet Earth, and it is here that the kingdom of God is now in the process of being built. This is not a mystical happening in space (heaven) but a transformation of energy to the efforts of peace, rather than war and hate. It will demand new technology, new systems of education, governments, civic and community standards, and the increased realization of the worth of every individual with ability granted to fulfill his potential and attain the excellence about which I have written.

Franklin D. Roosevelt initiated a "new deal" to stop breadlines during the depression of the thirties. The promise was a chicken in every pot and a car in every garage. Then came World War II in which most of the world was engulfed in a bitter struggle for survival. The "new deal" turned sour.

Lyndon Johnson, following John Kennedy, became the instigator of the "great society" in which segregation and injustice were supposed to vanish. However, since then some of the worst confrontations have taken place between the races, between the haves and the have-nots.

The dream has been impossible mainly because of polarization. Fragmentation has resulted from the erecting of walls and barriers which separate and divide. Little by little the will for union has been sacrificed to the gods of self-desire motivated by a vain pride to rule as creator rather than submit as creature.

Gadget minds have perfected deluxe dishwashers and air conditioners (all energy takers) but have failed to handle the complicated process of living together in homes, communities, and nations. Man has used his ingenuity to walk on the moon, while back on earth he sits in lonely, debilitating despair because he is still afraid. He has learned to transplant healthy organs for diseased parts of his anatomy but is fearful of transplanting thoughts and feelings to those of his own household. In an earth crowded with people, many still suffer in silent aloneness with eyes that see not, ears that hear not, and spirits that are broken.

America is supposed to be a religious country, but its churches suffer from self-righteousness, lack of vision, apathy, and refusal to face change. The early Christians didn't have to worry about raising money for ornate structures. They met in small groups—in homes and in out-of-the-way places due to the pressure exerted against them—but they were led by the Holy Spirit. Perhaps Christianity will again have to face such pressures if it is to survive.

I have been a churchgoing person all my life—over half a century—yet I am now convinced that cloistering together in a church sanctuary every Sunday (or Saturday) enjoying the service, the peace and respite from "the world," then going about business as usual will never build the kingdom or bring to pass the impossible dream.

Many church members are little more than facades—images of what they feel the Christian is supposed to be—how he is to act, what he is to say. But in this process the human element has been suppressed and the "new birth" spoken of by Jesus has been impossible. One must face himself as he is before he can become what Jesus referred to as the "new man."

Our churches need to become community centers that draw together men and women from all walks of life for specific purposes. I believe worship in the sanctuary is necessary, but that the many small groups springing up all over the country are getting people down to the basic level of expressions and feelings and bringing fantastic results.

It is perhaps a distinct characteristic of the American spirit to have a pioneer longing for new frontiers. Perhaps there is built in us all an urge to reach out for ways to improve our world. If we become overwhelmed by change, then all we can see is the now, and too often this causes us to be fearful to project into the future.

We wouldn't dare project a date and time for our dream to materialize. Yet many well known and innovative people have selected the year 2000 as the time when some kind of transformation will take place in our world.

One thing is certain. We have within our world the potential to build the impossible dream—a world with justice and integrity; yet we stand unwilling to risk what it will take to make the dream reality. If we fail it will not be for lack of resources or of viable alternatives but for lack of will. We need to turn from physical to spiritual frontiers. The exploration of these can be more intriguing, more exhilarating, and more liberating than any other kind.

To many youth Jesus may seem like superman. To those who have the will to delve deep into the God-man relationship and in the process encounter divinity, he is revealed as God in the person of the Son and the personality of the Holy Spirit. God is the ultimate creator and sustainer of all life. To fully comprehend this means we cease being the center of our world. We stop playing at being our own god, and recognize him as the center of our lives. Only when this happens can we really make progress in our climb to the peak of our mountain or in our search for meaning and fulfillment.

True power and glory come when we understand the supreme sacrifice on the Cross. It is not a fairy tale. We can't fantasize it away. It is stark reality. History records it, and men and women through every age of time have experienced the reality of the Cross and the joy of the Resurrection. There are actually only two ultimates—God and man. All else either enhances this relationship or restricts it. Too often Christianity has failed to carry this message with fidelity.

Martin D'Arcy, noted Catholic theologian, states his dream as Point Omega.

The universe itself is informed with psychic energy and somewhere on a line which passes through the axis of all possible universes is Point Omega at the center, as it were, of the whole space-time continuum from which pours out the spiritual force and radiance which certain mystics and saints can dimly comprehend. The goal of evolution is that all should comprehend and that finally humanity should open its parachute and perform an act of psychic union with Point Omega.—*Dialog with Myself.*

Perhaps we can refer to the peak of our crystal mountain as Point Omega.

P. Teilhard de Chardin has the strong hope "that a time will come when, without any loss of personalities, mankind by thinking alike in truth about universal peace and concord will reach one chorus of love and knowledge in Him who is Alpha and Omega."

If we climb up our crystal mountain, trudging in the footsteps of One who pointed the way, who continues to give direction, and whose promise is ultimate victory, we shall trust that promise and continue the journey confident of the joy that awaits.

There lies before us a world premier of experiences which can bring order out of chaos, love out of hate, peace out of war, and make the impossible dream reality.

There will come a time, when people will take delight in one another. When each will be a star to the other and when each will listen to his fellow man as to music. The free will walk upon the earth, men great in their freedom. They will walk with open hearts and the hearts of each will be pure of envy and greed . . . therefore all mankind will be without malice and there will be nothing to divorce the heart from reason. Then life will be one great service to man! His figure will be raised to lofty heights—for to free men all heights are attainable. Then we shall live in truth and freedom and in beauty.—From "Esperanza" by Maxim Gorki.

EPILOGUE

IT'S UP TO YOU NOW

I do not believe in a fate that falls on men however they act; but I do believe in a fate that falls on them unless they act.

There is a story called "The Death Machine" in which a man stumbles into a doctor's office and notices a machine by an open window. He fiddles with the dials and puts in his name, year, and day. The dials light up and the machine sends out a card that says, "You will be struck by lightning and killed at six o'clock tomorrow morning." The man is fascinated. Then he presses a button labeled, "death averted" and jumps five years in time. He sees that he will be rich and successful but that he will die in an airplane accident. Again he presses the "death averted" and goes ahead ten years. This time he has a lovely wife and happy children, but there is going to be a business disaster which causes him to commit suicide. Again he pushes the "death averted" and goes ahead fifteen years. He is so busy seeing what a wonderful happy life he could have that he doesn't notice the dawn

140

coming. He pays no attention to the open window and the rising wind. Suddenly, he is struck dead by lightning at six o'clock. He has been so busy trying to avert death that he fails to face the reality of life.

It's our decision now. What we as citizens of this planet have the potential to become lies in our hands. The plan has been given by One long ago. Whether we believe him to be savior, redeemer, master, teacher, rabbi, friend, Superstar or just a man, he did come into history. He did live and die and rise from a tomb, conquering death.

He came for one reason—to show us the way and to prove that we can live life victoriously even though it may mean pain, misunderstanding, ridicule, suffering, and perhaps a cross. He literally walked in our shoes—which is the only way he could actually know how we feel. I believe God became man so he could know our heartaches, frustrations, and our feeble attempts to be our own god, our feelings of loneliness and our frailties. He knew of our innate longing to belong, to be loved and needed. He was both human and divine, and within each of us there is divinity which constantly calls forth our best, given the climate and environment for growth and for living to our own greatest potential.

The senselessness of war and violence, the misuse of wealth and resources on the earth, the inherent right of everyone to live joyfully—all of these realities are sounding loud and clear to those who are open, aware, and have the consciousness to understand that man is spirit as well as physical. When we become aware of this, we have the awesome responsibility to do something about our awareness or face the dire consequences. Life is to be celebrated with joyous living, overcoming pain and suffering, being able to rise above the mundane, the misery and ugliness that often lie around us.

We can continue to push the "death averted" button just so long, then time runs out for us. At the peak of the crystal mountain lies that city of peace and love—not streets lined with gold nor a place where angels play harps but a visible world community where modern technology has presented us the opportunity and challenge to master machines, to be creative and innovative, to develop the nine-tenths of our minds that now lie untapped. Here the worth of each of us will be of ultimate value. Life will be productive, potentials will be realized, excellence will be achieved; and the zenith of our capabilities will spring forth like a rose ready to burst into bloom.

It's up to us. We'll bear the burden of failure or share in the glory of success. One thing is certain. We cannot long endure without hope and dreams. Eventually dreams must be realized or the vision fades. We are faced now with a choice. In fact, it is demanded of us. We must make the dream happen or face mass dissolution—perhaps annihilation.

The time has arrived for us to stand up and shout for the liberation of the whole human race. God will go with us in our climb, for we can never make it alone. We don't have to! I've had brief glimpses of the top of my mountain. Its beauty and majesty cannot be put into words. Nor can my feelings of completeness and wholeness which come with such vision.

My wish is that all may share in this aliveness and joy and be motivated in the quest to achieve this dream.

> *Existence is a strange bargain. Life owes us little; we owe it everything. The only true happiness comes from squandering ourselves for a purpose.* —John Mason Brown

BIBLIOGRAPHY

1. Leonard, George, *Transformation,* Delacorte, New York, 1972.
2. D'Arcy, Martin, *Dialogue with Myself,* Simon & Schuster, New York, 1966.
3. Tournier, Paul, *Place for You,* Harper & Row, New York, 1968.
4. Buttrick, George A., *Christ and History,* Abingdon, Nashville, Tennessee, 1963.
5. Frankl, Victor, *Will to Meaning,* New American Library, New York.
6. Gardner, John, *Excellence,* Harper & Row, New York, 1971.
7. Bach, Richard, *Jonathan Livingston Seagull,* Macmillan, New York, 1970.
8. Harris, Thomas A., *I'm OK—You're OK;* A Practical Guide to Transactional Analysis, Harper & Row, New York, 1969.
9. Powell, John, *Why Am I Afraid to Tell You Who I Am?,* Argus Communications, Niles, Illinois, 1969.
10. Fromm, Erich, *Escape from Freedom,* Holt, Rinehart & Winston, New York, 1941.
11. Rice, *Jesus Christ, Superstar,* Decca Records.